STEP-BY-STEP

Low Fat Balti Cookbook

STEP-BY-STEP

Low Fat Balti
Cookbook

SHEHZAD HUSAIN

Photographs by Ferguson Hill

AURA

Bismillah-hir-rahmaan-nir-raheem

Dedication

With love to my dear brother-in-law, Hashim Bhai

This edition published in 1997 by
Aura Books plc
Middlesex
England

© 1997 Anness Publishing Limited

Produced by
Anness Publishing Limited
Hermes House
88-89 Blackfriars Road
London SE1 8HA

ISBN 0 947793 03 8

A CIP catalogue record for this book is available from the British Library

Publisher: Joanna Lorenz
Editor: Linda Doeser
Designer: Brian Weldon
Stylist: Kay McGlone
Food for Photography: Kit Chan,
assisted by Hannah Mornement

Typeset by MC Typesetting, Rochester, Kent

For all recipes, quantities are given in both metric and imperial measures, and,
where appropriate, measures are also given in standard cups and spoons. Follow
one set, but not a mixture, because they are not interchangeable.

Printed in Hong Kong / China

CONTENTS

INTRODUCTION

Though traditionally the cuisines of India and Pakistan are not low in fat, it is surprisingly easy to create low fat Indian- and Pakistani-style meals that are high in flavour simply by adhering to a few dietary guidelines. Balti techniques particularly lend themselves to low fat cooking, and have the added advantages of being quick and easy.

Balti is essentially a way of cooking a wide range of curries rapidly on top of the stove over a high heat using a stir-fry method. It employs a wok-shaped cooking vessel with ring handles on either side, called a karahi. This is used extensively in the Indian subcontinent and made its way to the West via Pakistan's Multani community a decade or so ago. However, to enable a reduction in the amount of fat needed to achieve the stunningly flavoursome dishes in this book, a non-stick wok is recommended.

Balti food is fast, simple and delicious and should be fun to cook. You can enjoy preparing these dishes and eat them guilt-free. When you feel confident enough, use your own ideas to adapt recipes: you are the best judge of your palate. Happy cooking and eating!

Low Fat Cooking

There is now widespread agreement on what constitutes healthy eating, and the message is clear. We should all eat less fat, especially the saturated kind, less sugar, less salt and more fibre. We are advised to eat more fresh vegetables, fresh fruit and complex carbohydrate foods, such as rice, bread and pasta (preferably of whole-grain varieties), more fish, leaner meats and poultry without skin. The good thing about cooking chicken Indian/Pakistani style is that it is almost always cooked without the skin and amounts of meat are reduced because they are combined with vegetables or pulses.

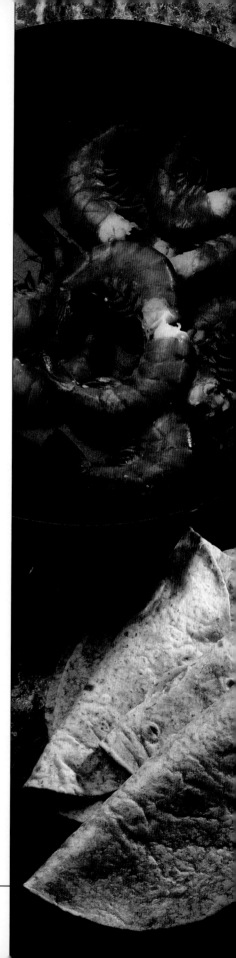

Whether they are specially created low fat dishes or not, all good Indian and Pakistani recipes always require well-trimmed lean cuts of meat, and for the recipes in this book where lamb is suggested, it is recommended that you use spring lamb, as not only is this leaner and quicker to cook, but also it has an excellent flavour which helps you achieve a more delicious end result.

An extensive range of fresh vegetables and whole foods, such as lentils and pulses, is an integral part of Indian/Pakistani cooking and every meal is served with either rice or bread and sometimes both. Brown varieties of both rice and flour are widely available.

The suggested changes in diet here are not designed to be dramatic. The recipes have been made as simple and uncomplicated as possible, but remember always to fry over a fairly low heat as you will be using far less fat than usual, which means that there is a higher chance of burning whatever you are frying.

Herbs and spices, which are also an essential part of Balti cooking, have two advantages: they do not contain fat and they add plenty of extra flavour and colour to dishes. Some recipes specify whole spices, such as cinnamon sticks, cardamom pods and cloves. If wished, these can be removed from the dish before serving.

Natural low fat yogurt is used in many of the recipes as a healthier alternative to cream. It is a wonderful tenderizer and gives curries a deliciously thick and creamy texture. Always beat the yogurt lightly with a fork first, then gradually add it to the pan placed over a low heat, stirring continuously, to prevent it from curdling.

Fromage frais, in its virtually fat-free version, is also used as a substitute for crème fraîche. Note: wherever fromage frais is specified in the ingredients in the recipes in this book, the virtually fat-free version is always intended. (All fromage frais has a fairly low fat content, but if you use a creamier version, the nutritional data will not apply.)

Fresh vegetables, seafood, chapatis and rice are the healthy constituents of a low fat Balti dish.

Spices

The spices used in a dish are integral to its flavour and aroma. One spice can completely alter the taste of a dish and a combination of several will also affect its colour and texture. The quantities of spices and salt specified in the recipes are merely a guide, so feel free to increase or decrease these as you wish. This is particularly true of fresh chillies and chilli powder: experiment with quantities, adding less than specified, if wished.

Cardamom pods
This spice is native to India, where it is considered to be the most prized spice after saffron. The pods can be used whole or the husks can be removed to release the seeds. They have a slightly pungent, but very aromatic taste. They come in three varieties: green, white and black. The green and white pods can be used for both sweet and savoury dishes or to flavour rice. The black pods are used only for savoury dishes (1).

Chillies – fresh and dried
These hot peppers are extremely fiery and should be used with caution. Much of the severe heat of fresh chillies is contained in the seeds, so the heat can be toned down by removing these before use. As a rule, dark green chillies tend to be hotter than light green ones and red chillies are usually milder still. However, this is not a hard-and-fast rule and it is always wise to be careful of an unfamiliar variety. Dried chillies can be used whole or coarsely crushed (2).

Chilli powder
Also known as cayenne pepper, this fiery ground spice should be used with caution. The heat varies from brand to brand, so adjust quantities to suit your tastebuds. Some brands include other spices and herbs, as well as ground chillies, and these may not be appropriate to the dish you are cooking. Always check the label carefully (3).

Cinnamon
One of the earliest known spices, cinnamon has an aromatic and sweet flavour. It is sold ready-ground and as sticks or bark (4).

Cloves
This spice is used to flavour many sweet and savoury dishes and is usually added whole (5).

Coriander seeds
This aromatic spice has a pungent, slightly lemony flavour. The seeds are used widely, either coarsely ground or in powdered form, in meat, fish and poultry dishes. Ground coriander, a brownish powder, is an important constituent of any mixture of curry spices (6).

Cumin
"White" cumin seeds are oval, ridged and greenish brown in colour. They have a strong aroma and flavour and can be used whole or ground. Ready-ground cumin powder is widely available. Black cumin seeds are dark and aromatic and are used to flavour curries and rice (7).

Fennel seeds
Very similar in appearance to cumin seeds, fennel seeds have a very sweet taste and are used to flavour certain curries. They can also be chewed as a mouth-freshener after a spicy meal (8).

Garam masala
This is a mixture of spices which can be made from freshly ground spices at home or purchased ready-made. There is no set recipe, but a typical mixture might include black cumin seeds, peppercorns, cloves, cinnamon and black cardamom pods (9).

Ginger
One of the most popular spices in India and also one of the oldest, fresh ginger is an important ingredient in many curries and is now widely available. The root should be plump with a fairly smooth skin, which is peeled off before use (10). Dried powdered ginger is a useful standby, but the flavour is not quite the same (11).

Mustard seeds – black and white
Round in shape and sharp in flavour, mustard seeds are used for flavouring curries, pickles and relishes (12).

Onion seeds
Black in colour and triangular in shape, these seeds are widely used in pickles and to flavour vegetable curries (13).

Paprika
A rust-red powder which has a sweetish, pungent taste and adds a good colour. Mild and hot varieties are available, although paprika is always much milder than chilli powder (14).

Peppercorns
Black peppercorns are sometimes used whole with other whole spices, such as cloves, cardamom pods and bay leaves, to flavour curries. Otherwise, whenever possible, use freshly ground or crushed black pepper (15).

Poppy seeds
Poppy seeds are usually toasted to bring out their flavour, and then used sprinkled over Indian breads (16).

Tamarind
This is a pulp-filled pod. It is used in paste form to add a sharp flavour to recipes, rather in the way western cooks use vinegar or lemon juice. It may be bought as a ready-made paste in jars or dried or compacted in packets (17).

Turmeric
This bright yellow, bitter-tasting spice is usually sold ground, although the fresh root is sometimes available. It is used mainly for additional colour rather than its flavour (18).

Herbs

Both fresh and dried herbs play an important part in the careful combinations of colour, flavour, aroma and texture which make up a Balti dish. Because the herbs have a minimal amount of cooking, they retain a marvellous intensity of flavour and fragrance.

Bay leaves
The large leaves of the bay laurel tree are one of the oldest herbs used in cookery. When used fresh they have a deliciously sweet flavour, but they keep very well in dried form (1).

Coriander
There is no substitute for fresh coriander and the more used the better, as it imparts an absolutely beautiful aroma and flavour. It is used both in cooking and sprinkled over dishes as an attractive garnish. It can be frozen successfully (2).

Curry leaves
Bright green and shiny, curry leaves are similar in appearance to bay leaves, but with a very different flavour. They can be bought dried and occasionally fresh from Asian stores. Fresh leaves freeze well (3).

Fenugreek
Fresh fenugreek is sold in bunches. It has very small leaves and is used to flavour both meat and vegetarian dishes. Always discard the stalks, which will impart an unpleasant bitterness to a dish if used. Fenugreek seeds are flat, extremely pungent and slightly bitter, so they should be used cautiously (4).

Mint
There are many different varieties of mint available and stronger-flavoured types tend to be used in Indian cooking. It is traditionally used in combination with lamb and to flavour some vegetables (5).

Lentils

There are many different types of lentils used in Indian cooking. Just four are used for the Balti dishes in this book and specific preparation and cooking instructions are given with each recipe.

Chana dhal
This is a round split yellow lentil, similar in appearance to the smaller moong dhal and the larger yellow split pea, which can be used as a substitute. It is used as a binding agent in some dishes and is widely available from Asian stores (1).

Masoor dhal
These split red lentils are actually orange in colour and turn a pale yellow when cooked. Whole brown lentils are a type of red lentil with the husk intact (2).

Toor dhal
A shiny split yellow lentil, toor dhal is similar in size to chana dhal (3).

Urid dhal
Also known as black gram, this lentil is similar in size to moong dhal and is available either with the blackish hull retained or removed (4).

Rice

Rice is served with almost every meal in India, so the Indians have created a variety of ways of cooking it, each quite distinctive. Plain boiled rice is an everyday accompaniment; for entertaining, it is combined with other ingredients to make a more interesting dish.

Whatever the dish, the aim is to produce dry, separate-grained rice that is cooked through yet still has some "bite" to it. The secret is to be reasonably precise about the amount of water you add to the rice, so that the rice can absorb all of it. Specific details are given with the individual recipes, but if you are just going to serve the rice plain, follow the instructions below.

Basmati rice, a long-grained, milled, white rice grown in both India and Pakistan, is the recommended type, because it cooks very well and gives an excellent finished result. Its name means "fragrant" and it has a distinctive and appealing aroma. Basmati rice is widely available from supermarkets and Asian food stores.

To cook plain boiled rice, always make sure you use a tight-fitting lid for your rice saucepan. If you do not have one that fits tightly enough, either wrap a tea towel around the lid or put some foil between the lid and the pan to make a snug fit. Try not to remove the lid until the rice is cooked. (The advantage of using just a lid is that you can tell when the rice is ready because steam begins to escape, visibly and rapidly.)

For four people, you will need 450g/1lb basmati rice. Wash it thoroughly until the water runs clear. Place the rice in a heavy-bottomed saucepan and add 5ml/1 tsp salt and 750ml/1¼ pints/3 cups of water. Bring to the boil, turn the heat very low and cover. Cook for 10–12 minutes.

Before serving, move the rice about gently with a slotted spoon to introduce air – the slotted spoon will prevent you from breaking up the grains, which would make the rice mushy.

As a rough guide, although it will vary according to individual appetites, allow about 75g/3oz rice per person.

Right:
Rice and chapatis provide complex carbohydrate foods, which form an important part of our diet.

TECHNIQUES

Pulping Fresh Ginger

Ginger pulp is specified in many of the Balti dishes and it can be time-consuming to peel and process fresh ginger root for each individual recipe. It's much easier to make the pulp in a large quantity and use it as needed.

Pulping Garlic

As with ginger pulp, it makes sense to prepare garlic pulp in reasonable quantities and store in the fridge or freezer until needed.

1 Peel off the tough skin using a small sharp knife or potato peeler.

2 Roughly chop the ginger into fairly small pieces.

1 Separate the garlic into cloves and peel off the skin.

2 Process the whole cloves in a food processor or blender.

3 Process the pieces in a food processor or blender, adding a little water if necessary to get the right consistency. Store in an airtight container in the fridge for 4–6 weeks or freeze in ice-cube trays kept for the purpose (they will absorb some of the smell from the ginger).

3 Freeze in ice-cube trays kept specially for the purpose. Put 5 ml/1 tsp in each compartment, freeze, remove from the tray and store in the freezer in a plastic bag. Alternatively store in an airtight container in the fridge for 4–6 weeks.

Freezing Fresh Coriander

There is no substitute for fresh coriander and the more used the better, as it imparts a beautiful flavour and aroma to Balti dishes. It is now readily available from most supermarkets and, more economically, from specialist Indian stores. If wished, you can buy a large quantity and freeze whatever you do not require immediately for future use.

Seeding and Chopping Chillies

Be sure to wash your hands after preparing chillies, to remove the stinging juice. Many of the recipes in this book specify two chillies, which will make the dish quite hot. Obviously you can reduce this number to taste. Also, the small fat chillies are milder than the long thin variety.

1 Cut off the roots and any thick stalks, but you can leave fine stalks.

1 Cut the chillies in half lengthways and remove the membranes and seeds.

2 Wash the leaves in cold water and leave in a strainer to drain.

3 When dry, chop the leaves and store them in plastic bags or airtight containers in the freezer. Do not defrost before using.

2 Cut the flesh lengthways into strips.

3 Cut the strips into small dice.

Chopping Onions

Many Balti dishes use chopped onions as an essential flavouring, and for stir-fried dishes it is important to keep the pieces even.

Slicing Onions

Use thin slices for stir-frying.

1 Peel the onion. Cut it in half with a large knife and set it cut side down on a board. Make lengthways vertical cuts along the onion, cutting almost but not quite through to the root.

2 Make two horizontal cuts from the stalk end towards the root, but not through it.

1 Peel the onion and cut it in half with a large knife.

2 Set it cut side down on a chopping board. Cut out a triangular piece of the core from the root end of each half.

3 Cut the onion crossways to form small, even dice.

3 Cut across each half in vertical slices.

Skinning and Chopping Tomatoes

It is sometimes recommended that you skin tomatoes before using them in a stir-fried dish.

1 Using a small sharp knife, cut a cross just through the skin at the bottom of each tomato.

2 Put the tomatoes in a bowl and pour over boiling water. Leave for 20–30 seconds until the skin splits. Drain and transfer to a bowl of cold water.

3 Peel off the skin and chop the flesh into even-size pieces.

Crushing Spices

All kinds of spices are used in Balti dishes to give the marvellous varieties of flavour. Some spices are used whole, but where they are crushed or ground, the best flavour will be obtained if you start off with whole spices and crush them as and when needed.

1 Crush whole spice in a coffee grinder. Alternatively use a pestle and mortar, especially for small quantities.

Chopping Herbs

Chop fresh herbs just before you need to add them to a dish.

1 Remove any thick stalks, then use a sharp knife to chop the leaves finely.

2 Alternatively use a herb chopper, also called a mezzaluna.

Browning Onions

The final colour and texture of a curry depends on how well you brown the onions during the first stage of cooking. This requires patience, especially as you will be cooking them in small quantities of oil.

Preparing Poultry and Meat

Poultry and meat for low fat dishes need to be trimmed of all skin and visible fat, so that only the lean part is used.

1 Heat 15 ml/1 tbsp oil in a non-stick wok or frying pan.

1 Always remove all the skin from chicken pieces.

2 Add the chopped or sliced onions, then reduce the heat slightly. Stir the onions only occasionally; excessive stirring will draw the moisture from them and inhibit the browning process.

3 Continue cooking until the onions are evenly golden brown.

2 Buy lean cuts of lamb, then trim off any visible fat.

3 Cut into even-size pieces for stir-frying. Cut the lamb into strips and the boned chicken into cubes.

Stir-frying

A non-stick wok or frying pan instead of the more traditional karahi is best for cooking low fat Balti dishes as it means that the quantity of oil used can be considerably reduced.

1 Always heat the wok or frying pan for a minute or so before adding the oil or any other ingredients.

2 When adding the oil, swirl it into the wok and allow it to heat before adding the next ingredients.

COOK'S TIP

Like karahis, woks are available in a range of sizes. It is important to use one that is large enough to allow the ingredients to move freely during stir-frying. A diameter of 35cm/14in is a good size for most family cooking. Make sure that the wok has deep sides.

3 When adding the first ingredients, reduce the heat a little. This will ensure that they are not overcooked or burnt by the time the remaining ingredients have been added.

4 Once all the ingredients have been added, quickly increase the heat to allow the dish to cook in the least possible time. This allows the ingredients to retain a crisp texture and prevents them from absorbing too much oil. Use a wooden spoon or non-stick slotted spoon to turn the ingredients as you stir-fry.

5 To clean the wok, wipe out the inside with kitchen paper where possible, keeping washing with detergent to the barest minimum.

Spinach with Mushrooms and Red Pepper

A tasty and nutritious vegetable, spinach cooked in this way is wonderful served with chapati.

Serves 4

INGREDIENTS
450g/1lb fresh or frozen spinach
30ml/2 tbsp corn oil
2 medium onions, diced
6–8 curry leaves
1.5ml/¼ tsp onion seeds
5ml/1 tsp garlic pulp
5ml/1 tsp ginger pulp
5ml/1 tsp chilli powder
5ml/1 tsp salt
7.5ml/1½ tsp ground coriander
1 large red pepper, seeded
   and sliced
115g/4oz mushrooms,
   roughly chopped
225g/8oz/1 cup fromage frais
30ml/2 tbsp fresh coriander leaves

mushrooms

spinach

chilli
powder

onions

pepper

fromage
frais

curry
leaves

coriander

onion
seeds

ginger
pulp

garlic
pulp

NUTRITIONAL NOTES
Per portion:
ENERGY 188 K Cals/778 K J **PROTEIN** 7.28g
FAT 11.57g **SATURATED FAT** 5.99g
CARBOHYDRATE 14.71g **FIBRE** 4.68g
ADDED SUGAR 0 **SALT** 0.66g

1 If using fresh spinach, blanch it briefly in boiling water and drain thoroughly. If using frozen spinach, thaw first, then drain. Set aside.

2 Heat the oil in a non-stick wok or frying pan and fry the onions with the curry leaves and the onion seeds for 1–2 minutes. Add the garlic, ginger, chilli powder, salt and ground coriander. Stir-fry for 2–3 minutes.

3 Add half the red pepper slices and all the mushrooms and continue to stir-fry for 2–3 minutes.

4 Add the spinach and stir-fry for 4–6 minutes. Finally, add the fromage frais and half the fresh coriander, followed by the remaining red pepper slices. Stir-fry for a further 2–3 minutes before serving, garnished with the remaining coriander.

Balti Mushrooms in a Creamy Garlic Sauce

This is a simple and delicious recipe which could be accompanied by any of the rice dishes from this book.

Serves 4

INGREDIENTS
350g/12oz button mushrooms
45ml/3 tbsp olive oil
1 bay leaf
3 garlic cloves, roughly chopped
2 green chillies, seeded
  and chopped
225g/8oz/1 cup fromage frais
15ml/1 tbsp chopped fresh mint
15ml/1 tbsp chopped
  fresh coriander
5ml/1 tsp salt
fresh mint and coriander leaves,
  to garnish

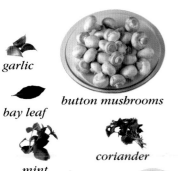

garlic

bay leaf *button mushrooms*

coriander

mint

green chillies

salt *fromage frais*

NUTRITIONAL NOTES
Per portion:

ENERGY 75 K Cals/314 K J **PROTEIN** 6.50g
FAT 3.38g **SATURATED FAT** 0.54g
CARBOHYDRATE 4.93g **FIBRE** 1.12g
ADDED SUGAR 0.01g
SALT 0.52g

1 Cut the mushrooms in half and set them aside.

2 Heat the oil in a non-stick wok or frying pan, then add the bay leaf, garlic and chillies and cook for about 1 minute.

COOK'S TIP
Cook the mushrooms for longer if you like them well cooked and browned.

3 Add the mushrooms. Stir-fry for about 2 minutes.

4 Remove from the heat and stir in the fromage frais followed by the mint, coriander and salt. Stir-fry for about 2 minutes, then transfer to a warmed serving dish and garnish with mint and coriander leaves.

Balti Sweetcorn with Cauliflower

This quick and tasty vegetable side dish is most easily made with frozen sweetcorn.

Serves 4

INGREDIENTS
30ml/2 tbsp corn oil
4 curry leaves
1.5ml/¼ tsp onion seeds
2 medium onions, diced
1 red chilli, seeded and diced
175g/6oz frozen sweetcorn
½ small cauliflower, cut into small florets
3–7 mint leaves

onions

cauliflower

curry leaves

red chilli

mint

onion seeds

sweetcorn

1 Heat the oil with the curry leaves and the onion seeds in a non-stick wok or frying pan for about 30 seconds.

2 Add the onions and fry them for 5–8 minutes until golden brown.

NUTRITIONAL NOTES
Per portion:
ENERGY 124 K Cals/519 K J **PROTEIN** 4.08g
FAT 3.89g **SATURATED FAT** 0.58g
CARBOHYDRATE 19.31g **FIBRE** 2.56g
ADDED SUGAR 0
SALT 0.12g

COOK'S TIP
It is best to cook this dish immediately before serving and eating, as the flavour tends to spoil if it is kept warm.

3 Add the chilli, sweetcorn and cauliflower and stir-fry for 5–8 minutes.

4 Finally, add the mint leaves and serve at once.

Balti Stir-fried Vegetables with Cashew Nuts

This versatile stir-fry will accommodate most other combinations of vegetables – you do not have to use the selection suggested here.

Serves 4

INGREDIENTS

2 medium carrots
1 medium red pepper, seeded
1 medium green pepper, seeded
2 courgettes
115g/4oz green beans, halved
1 medium bunch spring onions
15ml/1 tbsp virgin olive oil
4–6 curry leaves
2.5ml/½ tsp white cumin seeds
4 dried red chillies
10–12 cashew nuts
5ml/1 tsp salt
30ml/2 tbsp lemon juice
fresh mint leaves, to garnish

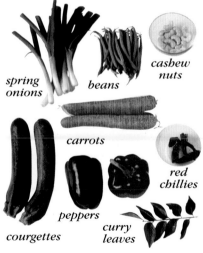

spring onions   *beans*   *cashew nuts*

carrots

red chillies

courgettes   *peppers*   *curry leaves*

NUTRITIONAL NOTES
Per portion:

ENERGY 98 K Cals/406 K J **PROTEIN** 4.04g
FAT 5.28g **SATURATED FAT** 0.88g
CARBOHYDRATE 10.25g **FIBRE** 3.94g
ADDED SUGAR 0.11g **SALT** 0.53g

1 Prepare the vegetables: cut the carrots, peppers and courgettes into matchsticks, halve the beans and chop the spring onions. Set aside.

2 Heat the oil in a non-stick wok or frying pan and fry the curry leaves, cumin seeds and dried chillies for about 1 minute.

3 Add the vegetables and nuts and stir them around gently. Add the salt and lemon juice. Continue to stir and cook for about 3–5 minutes.

4 Transfer to a serving dish and serve immediately. Garnish with mint leaves.

COOK'S TIP
If you are very short of time, use frozen mixed vegetables, which also work well in this dish.

Balti Toor Dhal with Spring Onion and Tomato

When cooked, toor dhal has a wonderfully rich texture, best appreciated if served with plain boiled rice. Fresh fenugreek leaves, available from Asian grocers, impart a stunning aroma.

Serves 4

INGREDIENTS
115g/4oz toor dhal
45ml/3 tbsp corn oil
1.5ml/¼ tsp onion seeds
1 medium bunch spring onions,
   roughly chopped
5ml/1 tsp garlic pulp
1.5ml/¼ tsp ground turmeric
7.5ml/1½ tsp ginger pulp
5ml/1 tsp chilli powder
30ml/2 tbsp fresh fenugreek leaves
5ml/1 tsp salt
150ml/¼ pint/⅔ cup water
6–8 cherry tomatoes
30ml/2 tbsp fresh coriander leaves
½ green pepper, seeded and sliced
15ml/1 tbsp lemon juice
shredded spring onion tops and
   fresh coriander leaves, to garnish

green pepper   tomatoes   toor dhal

onion seeds   spring onions

lemon juice

chilli powder   fenugreek

fresh coriander

ginger pulp   ground turmeric   garlic pulp   salt

1 Cook the dhal in boiling water until soft and mushy. Set aside.

2 Heat the oil with the onion seeds in a non-stick wok or frying pan for a few seconds until hot.

3 Add the dhal to the wok or frying pan and stir-fry for about 3 minutes.

4 Add the spring onions followed by the garlic, turmeric, ginger, chilli powder, fenugreek leaves and salt and continue to stir-fry for 5–7 minutes.

5 Pour in enough water to loosen the mixture.

NUTRITIONAL NOTES

Per portion:

ENERGY 137 K Cals/579 K J **PROTEIN** 8.27g
FAT 3.56g **SATURATED FAT** 0.55g
CARBOHYDRATE 19.62g **FIBRE** 2.49g
ADDED SUGAR 0
SALT 0.52g

COOK'S TIP

Any remaining fresh fenugreek leaves can be frozen in a plastic bag. If you cannot get fresh fenugreek, spinach can be used instead, but will produce a different taste.

6 Add the whole cherry tomatoes, coriander, green pepper and lemon juice. Serve garnished with shredded spring onion tops and coriander leaves.

Potatoes in Tomato Sauce

This curry makes an excellent accompaniment to almost any other savoury dish. Served with rice, it also makes a great vegetarian main course.

Serves 4

INGREDIENTS
10ml/2 tsp corn oil
1.5ml/¼ tsp onion seeds
4 curry leaves
2 medium onions, diced
400g/14oz can tomatoes
5ml/1 tsp ground cumin
7.5ml/1½ tsp ground coriander
5ml/1 tsp chilli powder
5ml/1 tsp ginger pulp
5ml/1 tsp garlic pulp
1.5ml/¼ tsp ground turmeric
5ml/1 tsp salt
15ml/1 tbsp lemon juice
15ml/1 tbsp chopped
  fresh coriander
2 medium potatoes, diced

tomatoes

onions

potatoes

turmeric

lemon
juice

onion
seeds

curry
leaves

fresh
coriander

salt

ground
cumin   garlic pulp   chilli powder

<u>NUTRITIONAL NOTES</u>
Per portion:
ENERGY 119 K Cals/502 K J **PROTEIN** 4.14g
FAT 2.27g **SATURATED FAT** 0.24g
CARBOHYDRATE 22.91g **FIBRE** 2.88g
ADDED SUGAR 0
SALT 0.54g

1 Heat the oil in a non-stick wok or frying pan and fry the onion seeds, curry leaves and onions over a medium heat.

2 Meanwhile place the canned tomatoes in a bowl and add the cumin, ground coriander, chilli powder, ginger, garlic, turmeric, salt, lemon juice and fresh coriander.

3 Pour this mixture into the wok and stir for about 1 minute to mix thoroughly with the onions.

4 Finally, add the potatoes, cover the pan and cook for 7–10 minutes over a low heat. Check whether the potatoes are cooked through, then serve.

COOK'S TIP
This curry is also delicious if you add a few cauliflower florets with the potatoes.

Balti Urid Dhal with Green and Red Chillies

The white urid dhal used in this recipe should ideally be soaked overnight as this makes it easier to cook. Serve with freshly made chapati.

Serves 4

INGREDIENTS
115g/4oz urid dhal
10ml/2 tsp low fat olive oil spread
10ml/2 tsp corn oil
1 bay leaf
2 onions, sliced
1 piece cinnamon bark
15ml/1 tbsp shredded fresh
   root ginger
2 garlic cloves
2 green chillies, seeded and
   sliced lengthways
2 red chillies, seeded and
   sliced lengthways
15ml/1 tbsp chopped fresh mint

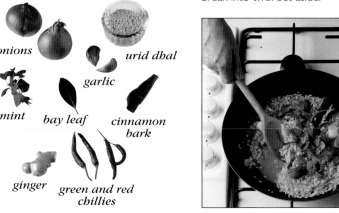

onions   urid dhal

        garlic

mint   bay leaf   cinnamon
                      bark

ginger   green and red
           chillies

NUTRITIONAL NOTES
Per portion:
ENERGY 159 K Cals/663 K J PROTEIN 8.65g
FAT 3.19g SATURATED FAT 0.51g
CARBOHYDRATE 24.38g FIBRE 1.15g
ADDED SUGAR 0.01g
SALT 0.03g

1 Soak the dhal overnight in enough cold water to cover. Boil in water until the individual grains are soft enough to break into two. Set aside.

2 Heat the low fat spread with the oil in a non-stick wok or frying pan over a medium heat. Fry the bay leaf with the onions and cinnamon bark.

3 Add the ginger, whole garlic cloves and half the green and red chillies.

COOK'S TIP
If you like your curries milder, replace some of the chillies with green or red peppers.

4 Drain almost all the water from the lentils. Add the lentils to the wok or frying pan, followed by the remaining green and red chillies and finally the fresh mint. Heat through briefly and serve.

Balti Potatoes with Aubergines

Using baby potatoes adds to the attractiveness of this dish. Choose the smaller variety of aubergines too, as they are far tastier than the large ones, which contain a lot of water and little flavour. Small aubergines are readily available from Asian grocers.

Serves 4

INGREDIENTS
10–12 baby potatoes
6 small aubergines
1 medium red pepper
15ml/1 tbsp corn oil
2 medium onions, sliced
4–6 curry leaves
2.5ml/½ tsp onion seeds
5ml/1 tsp crushed coriander seeds
2.5ml/1 tsp cumin seeds
5ml/1 tsp ginger pulp
5ml/1 tsp garlic pulp
5ml/1 tsp crushed dried red chillies
15ml/1 tbsp chopped
   fresh fenugreek
5ml/1 tsp chopped fresh coriander
15ml/1 tbsp natural low fat yogurt
fresh coriander leaves, to garnish

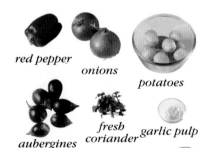

red pepper

onions

potatoes

aubergines   *fresh coriander*   *garlic pulp*

cumin seeds   *curry leaves*   *fenugreek*   *red chillies*

ginger pulp   *onion seeds*   *yogurt*   *coriander seeds*

1 Cook the unpeeled potatoes in boiling water until just soft. Set aside.

2 Cut the aubergines into quarters.

3 Cut the pepper in half, remove the seeds, then slice the flesh into strips.

4 Heat the oil in a non-stick wok or frying pan and fry the onions, curry leaves, onion seeds, crushed coriander seeds and cumin seeds until the onions are a soft golden brown.

5 Add the ginger, garlic, crushed chillies and fenugreek, followed by the aubergines and potatoes. Stir everything together and cover with a lid. Lower the heat and cook for 5–7 minutes.

NUTRITIONAL NOTES

Per portion:

ENERGY 183 K Cals/773 K J **PROTEIN** 5.75g
FAT 4.42g **SATURATED FAT** 0.7g
CARBOHYDRATE 33.02g **FIBRE** 5.43g
ADDED SUGAR 0
SALT 0.03g

COOK'S TIP

To prevent curdling it is always best to whisk the yogurt before adding to a hot dish.

6 Remove the lid, add the fresh coriander followed by the natural yogurt and stir well. Serve garnished with coriander leaves.

Carrot and Cauliflower Stir-fry

The carrots are thinly sliced, which means that they cook quickly. This dish has a crunchy texture with only a few whole spices.

Serves 4

INGREDIENTS
2 large carrots
1 small cauliflower
15ml/1 tbsp olive oil
1 bay leaf
2 cloves
1 small cinnamon stick
2 cardamom pods
3 black peppercorns
5ml/1 tsp salt
50g/2oz frozen peas
10ml/2 tsp lemon juice
15ml/1 tbsp chopped
  fresh coriander
fresh coriander leaves, to garnish

frozen peas   *lemon juice*   *salt*

cinnamon   *cardamom*   *peppercorns*
cloves   *bay leaf*

cauliflower   *carrots*
fresh coriander

NUTRITIONAL NOTES
Per portion:

ENERGY 84 K Cals/349 K J **PROTEIN** 3.91g
FAT 3.75g **SATURATED FAT** 0.6g
CARBOHYDRATE 9.05g **FIBRE** 3.67g
ADDED SUGAR 0
SALT 0.5 g

1 Cut the carrots into thin batons about 2.5cm/1 in long. Separate the cauliflower into small florets.

2 Heat the oil in a non-stick wok or frying pan and add the bay leaf, cloves, cinnamon, cardamoms and peppercorns. Stir-fry over a medium heat for 30–35 seconds, then add the salt.

3 Next add the carrot and cauliflower and continue to stir-fry for 3–5 minutes.

4 Add the peas, lemon juice and chopped coriander and cook for a further 2–3 minutes. Serve garnished with the whole coriander leaves.

Beans with Sweetcorn

Frozen French beans are useful for this, as they are quick to cook. The dish makes an excellent vegetable accompaniment to the fish and meat dishes in this book.

Serves 4

INGREDIENTS
15ml/1 tbsp olive oil
1.5ml/¼ tsp mustard seeds
1 medium red onion, diced
50g/2oz frozen sweetcorn
50g/2oz canned red kidney beans
175g/6oz frozen French beans
1 medium red chilli, seeded
  and diced
1 garlic clove, chopped
2.5 cm/1 in piece fresh root ginger,
  finely chopped
15ml/1 tbsp chopped
  fresh coriander
5ml/1 tsp salt
1 medium tomato, seeded and
  diced, to garnish

sweetcorn | red kidney beans | French beans
onion | coriander
tomato | salt
red chilli
ginger | garlic | mustard seeds

NUTRITIONAL NOTES
Per portion:
ENERGY 84 K Cals/349 K J **PROTEIN** 2.96g
FAT 3.44g **SATURATED FAT** 0.50g
CARBOHYDRATE 11.13g **FIBRE** 2.70g
ADDED SUGAR 0 **SALT** 0.58g

1 Heat the oil in a non-stick wok or frying pan for about 30 seconds, then add the mustard seeds and onion. Fry for about 2 minutes.

2 Add the sweetcorn, the drained kidney beans and French beans. Stir-fry for about 3–5 minutes.

3 Add the chilli, garlic and ginger, coriander and salt and stir-fry for 2–3 minutes.

4 Remove the pan from the heat. Transfer to a serving dish and garnish with the diced tomato.

Spiced Potatoes and Tomatoes

Diced potatoes are cooked gently in a fresh tomato sauce, which is flavoured with curry leaves and green chillies.

NUTRITIONAL NOTES

Per portion:

ENERGY 188 K Cals/790 K J PROTEIN 8.54 g
FAT 7.62 g SATURATED FAT 1.66 g
CARBOHYDRATE 23.40 g FIBRE 3.10 g
ADDED SUGAR 0.01g
SALT 0.57g

Serves 4

INGREDIENTS
2 medium potatoes
15ml/1 tbsp olive oil
2 medium onions, finely chopped
4 curry leaves
1.5ml/¼ tsp onion seeds
1 green chilli, seeded and chopped
4 tomatoes, sliced
5ml/1 tsp ginger pulp
5ml/1 tsp garlic pulp
5ml/1 tsp chilli powder
5ml/1 tsp ground coriander
5ml/1 tsp lemon juice
15ml/1 tbsp chopped
    fresh coriander
salt
3 hard-boiled eggs, to garnish

 potatoes   *onions*

 tomatoes   *onion seeds*   *chilli powder*

curry leaves   *green chilli*

lemon juice   *garlic pulp*   *ground coriander*

eggs   *fresh coriander*   *ginger pulp*

1 Peel and dice the potatoes.

2 Heat the oil in a non-stick wok or frying pan and stir-fry the onions, curry leaves, onion seeds and green chilli for about 40 seconds.

3 Add the tomatoes and cook for about 2 minutes over a low heat.

4 Add the ginger and garlic, chilli powder, ground coriander and salt to taste. Continue to stir-fry for 1–2 minutes, then add the potatoes and cook, covered, over a low heat for 5–7 minutes until the potatoes are tender.

5 Add the lemon juice and fresh coriander and stir to mix together.

6 Shell the hard-boiled eggs, cut into quarters and add as a garnish to the finished dish.

Cod in a Tomato Sauce

The cod is lightly dusted with spices and a little cornflour before being added to the tomato sauce. Mashed potatoes are the perfect accompaniment, although roast potatoes and rice are also good.

Serves 4

INGREDIENTS
30ml/2 tbsp cornflour
5ml/1 tsp salt
5ml/1 tsp garlic powder
5ml/1 tsp chilli powder
5ml/1 tsp ginger powder
5ml/1 tsp ground fennel seeds
5ml/1 tsp ground coriander
2 medium cod fillets, each cut into
    2 pieces
15ml/1 tbsp corn oil
mashed potatoes, to serve

FOR THE SAUCE
30ml/2 tbsp tomato purée
5ml/1 tsp garam masala
5ml/1 tsp chilli powder
5ml/1 tsp garlic pulp
5ml/1 tsp ginger pulp
2.5ml/½ tsp salt
175ml/6 fl oz/⅔ cup water
15ml/1 tbsp corn oil
1 bay leaf
3–4 black peppercorns
1 cm/½ in cinnamon bark
15ml/1 tbsp chopped fresh
    fresh coriander
15ml/1 tbsp chopped fresh mint

cod fillets

fresh
coriander

peppercorns bay
leaf cinnamon
bark

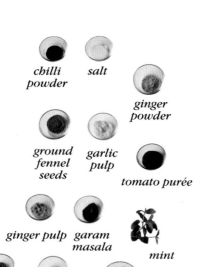

chilli
powder salt

ginger
powder

ground
fennel
seeds garlic
pulp

tomato purée

ginger pulp garam
masala

mint

ground
coriander garlic
powder

cornflower

1 Mix together the cornflour, salt, garlic powder, chilli powder, ginger powder, ground fennel seeds and ground coriander seeds.

2 Pour this mixture over the 4 cod fillets and make sure that they are well coated.

3 Preheat the grill to very hot, reduce the heat to medium and place the fish under the grill. After about 5 minutes brush the cod with the oil. Turn the cod over and repeat the process. Grill for a further 5 minutes, check that the fish is cooked through and set aside.

4 Make the sauce by mixing together the tomato purée, garam masala, chilli powder, garlic, ginger, salt and water. Set aside.

COOK'S TIP
Fresh or frozen fish can be used for this dish.

NUTRITIONAL NOTES

Per portion:

ENERGY 122 K Cals/509 K J **PROTEIN** 12.70g
FAT 6.65g **SATURATED FAT** 0.89g
CARBOHYDRATE 4.73g **FIBRE** 0.48g
ADDED SUGAR 0
SALT 0.8g

5 Heat the oil in a non-stick wok or frying pan and add the bay leaf, peppercorns and cinnamon. Pour the sauce into the wok and reduce the heat to low. Bring gently to the boil, stirring occasionally, and simmer for about 5 minutes. Gently slide the pieces of fish into this mixture and cook for a further 2 minutes.

6 Finally, add the fresh coriander and mint and serve with mashed potatoes.

Cod with a Spicy Mushroom Sauce

The cod is grilled before it is added to the sauce to prevent it from breaking up during cooking.

Serves 4

INGREDIENTS
4 cod fillets
15ml/1 tbsp lemon juice
15ml/1 tbsp olive oil
1 medium onion, chopped
1 bay leaf
4 black peppercorns, crushed
115g/4oz mushrooms
175ml/6fl oz/⅔ cup natural low
   fat yogurt
5ml/1 tsp ginger pulp
5ml/1 tsp garlic pulp
2.5ml/½ tsp garam masala
2.5ml/½ tsp chilli powder
5ml/1 tsp salt
15ml/1 tbsp fresh coriander leaves,
   to garnish
lightly cooked green beans, to serve

ginger pulp   onion

lemon juice   cod fillets   mushrooms

chilli powder   bay leaf

garam masala   garlic pulp   fresh coriander   yogurt

NUTRITIONAL NOTES
Per portion:
ENERGY 170 K Cals/715 K J   **PROTEIN** 25.80g
FAT 4.32g   **SATURATED FAT** 0.79g
CARBOHYDRATE 7.67g   **FIBRE** 1.00g
ADDED SUGAR 0   **SALT** 0.61g

1 Remove the skin and any bones from the cod fillets. Sprinkle with lemon juice, then grill under a preheated grill for about 5 minutes on each side. Remove from the heat and set aside.

2 Heat the oil in a non-stick wok or frying pan and fry the onion with the bay leaf and peppercorns for 2–3 minutes. Lower the heat, then add the mushrooms and stir-fry for 4–5 minutes.

3 In a bowl mix together the yogurt, ginger and garlic, garam masala, chilli powder and salt. Pour this over the onions and stir-fry for 3 minutes.

4 Add the cod to the sauce and cook for a further 2 minutes. Serve garnished with the coriander and accompanied by lightly cooked green beans.

Stir-fried Vegetables with Monkfish

Monkfish is a rather expensive fish, but ideal to use in stir-fry recipes as it is quite tough and does not break easily.

Serves 4

INGREDIENTS
30ml/2 tbsp corn oil
2 medium onions, sliced
5ml/1 tsp garlic pulp
5ml/1 tsp ground cumin
5ml/1 tsp ground coriander
5ml/1 tsp chilli powder
175g/6 oz monkfish, cut into cubes
30ml/2 tbsp fresh fenugreek leaves
2 tomatoes, seeded and sliced
1 courgette, sliced
15ml/1 tbsp lime juice
salt

onions
courgette   monkfish

tomatoes   fenugreek   lime juice

chilli powder   ground cumin
ground coriander   garlic pulp

NUTRITIONAL NOTES
Per portion:
ENERGY 86 K Cals/360 K J PROTEIN 9.18g
FAT 2.38g SATURATED FAT 0.35g
CARBOHYDRATE 8.30g FIBRE 1.87g
ADDED SUGAR 0.02g
SALT 0.27g

1 Heat the oil in a non-stick wok or frying pan and fry the onions over a low heat until soft.

2 Meanwhile mix together the garlic, cumin, coriander and chilli powder. Add this spice mixture to the onions and stir for about 1 minute.

COOK'S TIP
Try to use monkfish for this recipe, but if it is not available, either cod or prawns make a suitable substitute.

3 Add the fish and continue to stir-fry for 3–5 minutes until the fish is well cooked through.

4 Add the fenugreek, tomatoes and courgette, followed by salt to taste, and stir-fry for a further 2 minutes. Sprinkle with lime juice before serving.

Prawn and Vegetable Balti

A simple and delicious accompaniment to many other Balti dishes.

Serves 4

INGREDIENTS
175g/6 oz frozen cooked,
  peeled prawns
30ml/2 tbsp corn oil
1.5ml/¼ tsp onion seeds
4–6 curry leaves
115g/4oz frozen peas
115g/4oz frozen sweetcorn
1 large courgette, sliced
1 medium red pepper, seeded and
  roughly diced
5ml/1 tsp crushed coriander seeds
5ml/1 tsp crushed dried red chillies
15ml/1 tbsp lemon juice
salt
15ml/1 tbsp fresh coriander leaves,
  to garnish

prawns   peas   sweetcorn

red pepper   curry leaves

courgette

fresh coriander

onion seeds   dried red chillies   coriander seeds

lemon juice

NUTRITIONAL NOTES
Per portion:
ENERGY 134 K Cals/566 K J   PROTEIN 13.94g
FAT 3.04g   SATURATED FAT 0.51g
CARBOHYDRATE 14.03g   FIBRE 2.96g
ADDED SUGAR 0
SALT 1.03g

COOK'S TIP
The best way to crush whole seeds is to use an electric spice grinder or a small marble pestle and mortar.

1 Thaw the prawns and drain them of any excess liquid.

2 Heat the oil with the onion seeds and curry leaves in a non-stick wok or frying pan.

3 Add the prawns to the wok and stir-fry until the liquid has evaporated.

4 Next add the peas, sweetcorn, courgette and red pepper. Continue to stir for 3–5 minutes.

5 Finally, add the coriander seeds, chillies, salt to taste and lemon juice.

6 Serve immediately, garnished with fresh coriander leaves.

Grilled King Prawn Bhoona

The unusual and delicious flavour of this dish is achieved by grilling the prawns to give them a char-grilled taste and then adding them to fried onions and peppers.

Serves 4

INGREDIENTS
45ml/3 tbsp natural low fat yogurt
5ml/1 tsp paprika
5ml/1 tsp ginger pulp
12–14 frozen cooked king prawns, thawed and peeled
15ml/1 tbsp corn oil
3 medium onions, sliced
2.5ml/½ tsp fennel seeds, crushed
1 cinnamon bark
5ml/1 tsp garlic pulp
5ml/1 tsp chilli powder
1 medium yellow pepper, seeded and roughly chopped
1 medium red pepper, seeded and roughly chopped
salt
15ml/1 tbsp fresh coriander leaves, to garnish

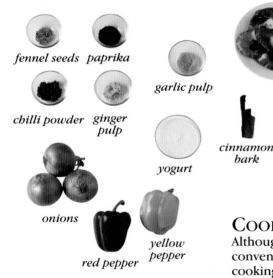

fennel seeds *paprika*

garlic pulp

king prawns

chilli powder *ginger pulp*

cinnamon bark

yogurt

fresh coriander

onions

red pepper *yellow pepper*

1 Blend together the yogurt, paprika, ginger, and salt to taste. Pour this mixture over the prawns and leave to marinate for 30–45 minutes.

COOK'S TIP
Although frozen coriander is convenient and good to use in cooking, the fresh herb is more suitable for garnishes.

2 Meanwhile, heat the oil in a non-stick wok or frying pan and fry the onions with the fennel seeds and the cinnamon bark.

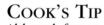

3 Lower the heat and add the garlic and chilli powder.

4 Add the peppers and stir-fry gently for 3–5 minutes.

NUTRITIONAL NOTES

Per portion:

ENERGY 132 K Cals/552 K J **PROTEIN** 9.97g
FAT 3.94g **SATURATED FAT** 0.58g
CARBOHYDRATE 15.93g **FIBRE** 3.11g
ADDED SUGAR 0.02g
SALT 0.79g

5 Remove from the heat and transfer to a serving dish, discarding the cinnamon bark.

6 Preheat the grill and turn the heat to medium. Put the prawns in a grill pan or flameproof dish and place under the grill to darken their tops and achieve a char-grilled effect. Add the prawns to the onion mixture, garnish with the coriander and serve.

King Prawns with Onion and Curry Leaves

An excellent partner for this prawn dish is Basmati Rice with Potatoes.

Serves 4

INGREDIENTS
3 medium onions
15ml/1 tbsp corn oil
6–8 curry leaves
1.5ml/¼ tsp onion seeds
1 green chilli, seeded and diced
1 red chilli, seeded and diced
12–14 frozen cooked king prawns,
   thawed and peeled
5ml/1 tsp shredded fresh
   root ginger
5ml/1 tsp salt
15ml/1 tbsp fresh fenugreek leaves

onions

king prawns

onion seeds   *fresh fenugreek*

root ginger   *curry leaves*   *salt*

green and red chillies

NUTRITIONAL NOTES
Per portion:
ENERGY 97 K Cals/403 K J   **PROTEIN** 8.03g
FAT 3.29g   **SATURATED FAT** 0.45g
CARBOHYDRATE 9.38g   **FIBRE** 1.58g
ADDED SUGAR 0.01g
SALT 0.94g

1 Slice the onions.

2 Heat the oil in a non-stick wok or frying pan and fry the onions with the curry leaves and onion seeds for about 3 minutes.

COOK'S TIP
A good-quality virgin olive oil can be used instead of corn oil, if preferred.

3 Add the diced green and red chillies, followed by the prawns. Cook for about 5–7 minutes before adding the ginger and salt.

4 Finally, add the fenugreek leaves, cover and cook for a further 2–3 minutes before serving.

Prawn and Mangetout Stir-fry

It is always a good idea to keep some frozen prawns in stock, as they are always handy for a quick stir-fry like this one. Serve with plain boiled rice or chapatis.

Serves 4

INGREDIENTS
15ml/1 tbsp corn oil
2 medium onions, diced
15ml/1 tbsp tomato purée
5ml/1 tsp Tabasco sauce
5ml/1 tsp lemon juice
5ml/1 tsp ginger pulp
5ml/1 tsp garlic pulp
5ml/1 tsp chilli powder
5ml/1 tsp salt
15ml/1 tbsp chopped
   fresh coriander
175g/6 oz frozen cooked peeled
   prawns, thawed
12 mangetouts, halved

Tabasco sauce
onions
prawns
ginger pulp
salt
fresh coriander
garlic pulp
mangetouts
tomato purée
chilli powder

NUTRITIONAL NOTES
Per portion:
ENERGY 108 K Cals/451 K J **PROTEIN** 11.88g
FAT 3.48g **SATURATED FAT** 0.49g
CARBOHYDRATE 7.96g **FIBRE** 1.60g
ADDED SUGAR 0
SALT 1.22g

1 Heat the oil in a non-stick wok or frying pan and fry the onions over a low heat for about 2 minutes, or until they are golden brown.

2 Meanwhile mix the tomato purée with 30ml/2 tbsp water in a bowl, then stir in the Tabasco sauce, lemon juice, ginger pulp, garlic pulp, chilli powder and salt and blend well.

3 Lower the heat, pour the sauce over the onions and stir-fry.

4 Add the coriander, prawns and mangetouts and stir-fry for 5–7 minutes, or until the sauce is thick. Serve hot.

King Prawn Korma

This korma has a light, mild, creamy texture, and makes a good introduction to Balti cuisine for people who claim not to like spicy food. The coconut milk makes the sauce creamy and rich.

NUTRITIONAL NOTES

Per portion:

ENERGY 90 K Cals/376 K J **PROTEIN** 7.25g
FAT 5.55g **SATURATED FAT** 1.95g
CARBOHYDRATE 3.21g **FIBRE** 0.37g
ADDED SUGAR 0.52g
SALT 0.66g

Serves 4

INGREDIENTS
10–12 frozen cooked king prawns, thawed and peeled if necessary
45ml/3 tbsp natural low fat yogurt
45ml/3 tbsp fromage frais
5ml/1 tsp ground paprika
5ml/1 tsp garam masala
15ml/1 tbsp tomato purée
45ml/3 tbsp coconut milk
5ml/1 tsp chilli powder
150ml/¼ pint/⅔ cup water
15ml/1 tbsp corn oil
5ml/1 tsp garlic pulp
5ml/1 tsp ginger pulp
½ piece cinnamon bark
2 green cardamom pods
salt
15ml/1 tbsp chopped fresh coriander, to garnish

tomato purée

chilli powder

cardamom

cinnamon bark

prawns

garlic pulp

fromage frais

coconut milk

ginger pulp

garam masala

ground paprika

fresh coriander

yogurt

1 Drain the prawns to ensure that all excess liquid is removed.

2 Place the yogurt, fromage frais, paprika, garam masala, tomato purée, coconut milk, chilli powder and water in a bowl.

3 Blend everything together well and set aside.

4 Heat the oil in a non-stick wok or frying pan, add the garlic, ginger, cinnamon, cardamoms and salt to taste and fry over a low heat.

5 Pour in the spice mixture and bring to the boil, stirring occasionally.

6 Add the prawns to this and continue to stir-fry until the sauce is quite thick. Serve garnished with the chopped coriander.

COOK'S TIP

Paprika adds a good rich colour to the curry without extra heat.

Kashmiri Chicken Curry

This mild yet flavoursome dish is given a special lift by the addition of apples.

NUTRITIONAL NOTES
Per portion:
ENERGY 237 K Cals/994 K J **PROTEIN** 24.78g
FAT 8.25g **SATURATED FAT** 1.31g
CARBOHYDRATE 17.21g **FIBRE** 2.88g
ADDED SUGAR 0
SALT 0.6g

Serves 4

INGREDIENTS
10ml/2 tsp corn oil
2 medium onions, diced
1 bay leaf
2 cloves
2.5cm/1in cinnamon stick
4 black peppercorns
1 baby chicken, about 675g/1½lb, skinned and cut into 8 pieces
5ml/1 tsp garam masala
5ml/1 tsp ginger pulp
5ml/1 tsp garlic pulp
5ml/1 tsp salt
5ml/1 tsp chilli powder
15ml/1 tbsp ground almonds
150ml/¼ pint/⅔ cup natural low fat yogurt
2 green eating apples, peeled, cored and roughly sliced
15ml/1 tbsp chopped fresh coriander
15g/½oz flaked almonds, lightly toasted, and fresh coriander leaves, to garnish

onions

apples   *baby chicken*

garlic pulp   *garam masala*   *yogurt*

ginger pulp *bay leaf*

fresh coriander

chilli powder *flaked almonds* *ground almonds*

peppercorns   *cloves*

cinnamon stick

salt

1 Heat the oil in a non-stick wok or frying pan and fry the onions with the bay leaf, cloves, cinnamon and peppercorns for about 3–5 minutes.

2 Add the chicken pieces and continue to stir-fry for at least 3 minutes.

3 Lower the heat and add the garam masala, ginger, garlic, salt, chilli powder and ground almonds and continue to stir for 2–3 minutes.

4 Pour in the yogurt and stir for a couple more minutes.

5 Add the apples and chopped coriander, cover and cook for about 10–15 minutes.

6 Check that the chicken is cooked through and serve immediately, garnished with the flaked almonds and whole coriander leaves.

Balti Minced Chicken with Green and Red Chillies

Minced chicken is seldom cooked in Indian or Pakistani homes. However it works very well in this recipe.

Serves 4

INGREDIENTS
275g/10oz boned and cubed
  skinless chicken breast
2 thick red chillies
3 thick green chillies
45ml/3 tbsp corn oil
6 curry leaves
3 medium onions, sliced
7.5ml/1½ tsp garlic pulp
7.5ml/1½ tsp ground coriander
7.5ml/1½ tsp ginger pulp
5ml/1 tsp chilli powder
5ml/1 tsp salt
15ml/1 tbsp lemon juice
30ml/2 tbsp chopped fresh
  coriander leaves
chapatis and lemon wedges, to serve

onions

curry leaves

chicken

green chillies

salt

lemon juice

red chillies

fresh coriander

garlic pulp

ginger pulp

ground coriander

chilli powder

1 Boil the chicken cubes in water for about 10 minutes until soft and cooked through. Drain.

2 Place the chicken in a food processor to mince.

3 Cut the chillies in half lengthways and remove the seeds, if desired. Cut the flesh into strips.

4 Heat the oil in a non-stick wok or frying pan and fry the curry leaves and onions until the onions are a soft golden brown. Lower the heat and add the garlic pulp, ground coriander, ginger pulp, chilli powder and salt.

5 Add the minced chicken and stir-fry for 3–5 minutes.

NUTRITIONAL NOTES

Per portion:

ENERGY 152 K Cals/637 K J **PROTEIN** 19.11g
FAT 4.1 g **SATURATED FAT** 0.62g
CARBOHYDRATE 10.94g **FIBRE** 1.80g
ADDED SUGAR 0.01g
SALT 0.54g

COOK'S TIP

Taste this dish during cooking as it is quite mild, especially if you seed the chillies, and may need additional spices to suit some palates.

6 Add the lemon juice, the chilli strips and most of the fresh coriander leaves. Stir for a further 3–5 minutes, then serve, garnished with the remaining coriander leaves and accompanied by chapatis and lemon wedges.

Ginger Chicken Wings

Fresh ginger pulp is used in the marinade and this dish is also garnished with shredded ginger. Try to buy skinned chicken wings, as it is very difficult to skin them yourself.

Serves 4

INGREDIENTS
10–12 chicken wings, skinned
175ml/6 fl oz/⅔ cup natural low
    fat yogurt
7.5ml/1½ tsp ginger pulp
5ml/1 tsp salt
5ml/1 tsp Tabasco sauce
15ml/1 tbsp tomato ketchup
5ml/1 tsp garlic pulp
15ml/1 tbsp lemon juice
15ml/1 tbsp fresh coriander leaves
15ml/1 tbsp corn oil
2 medium onions, sliced
15ml/1 tbsp shredded fresh
    root ginger

onions

ketchup

fresh
coriander

Tabasco sauce

chicken
wings

root ginger

garlic pulp

ginger
pulp   lemon
        juice   salt   yogurt

NUTRITIONAL NOTES
Per portion:
ENERGY 224 K Cals/936 K J **PROTEIN** 24.33g
FAT 9.00g **SATURATED FAT** 2.23g
CARBOHYDRATE 12.07g **FIBRE** 1.24g
ADDED SUGAR 0.57g
SALT 0.66g

1 Place the chicken wings in a bowl. Pour the yogurt into a separate bowl along with the ginger pulp, salt, Tabasco sauce, ketchup, garlic pulp, lemon juice and half the coriander. Whisk everything together, pour over the chicken wings and mix well.

2 Heat the oil in a non-stick wok or frying pan and fry the onions until soft.

3 Pour in the chicken wings and cook over a medium heat, stirring occasionally, for 10–15 minutes.

4 Add the remaining coriander and the shredded ginger and serve hot.

COOK'S TIP
You can substitute drumsticks or other chicken portions for the wings in this recipe, but remember to increase the cooking time.

Balti Chicken in Orange and Black Pepper Sauce

Use virtually fat-free fromage frais to give this sauce a rich, creamy flavour.

Serves 4

INGREDIENTS
225g/8oz fromage frais
50ml/2 fl oz/¼ cup natural low
    fat yogurt
120ml/4 fl oz/½ cup orange juice
7.5ml/1½ tsp ginger pulp
5ml/1 tsp garlic pulp
5ml/1 tsp freshly ground
    black pepper
5ml/1 tsp salt
5ml/1 tsp ground coriander
1 baby chicken, about 675g/1½lb,
    skinned and cut into 8 pieces
15ml/1 tbsp corn oil
1 bay leaf
1 large onion, chopped
15ml/1 tbsp fresh mint leaves
1 green chilli, seeded and chopped

*orange
juice*

*ginger
pulp*　　　*chicken*

onion

mint

*green
chilli*　　*garlic
pulp*　*fromage
frais*

bay leaf

NUTRITIONAL NOTES
Per portion:

ENERGY 199 K Cals/836 K J **PROTEIN** 26.07g
FAT 5.11g **SATURATED FAT** 1.06g
CARBOHYDRATE 13.20g **FIBRE** 1.02g
ADDED SUGAR 1.20g **SALT** 0.6g

1 In a bowl, whisk together the fromage frais, yogurt, orange juice, ginger, garlic, pepper, salt and coriander.

2 Pour this over the chicken and set aside for 3–4 hours.

COOK'S TIP
If you prefer the taste of curry leaves, you can use them instead of the bay leaf, but you need to double the quantity.

3 Heat the oil with the bay leaf in a non-stick wok or frying pan and fry the onion until soft.

4 Pour in the chicken mixture and stir-fry for 3–5 minutes over a medium heat. Lower the heat, cover with a lid and cook for 7–10 minutes, adding a little water if the sauce is too thick. Finally add the fresh mint and chilli and serve.

Balti Chicken with Panir and Peas

Rather an unusual combination, but it really works well. Serve with plain boiled rice.

Serves 4

INGREDIENTS
1 baby chicken, about 675g/1½ lb
30ml/2 tbsp tomato purée
45ml/3 tbsp natural low fat yogurt
7.5ml/1½ tsp garam masala
5ml/1 tsp garlic pulp
5ml/1 tsp ginger pulp
pinch of ground cardamom
15ml/1 tbsp chilli powder
1.5ml/¼ tsp ground turmeric
5ml/1 tsp salt
5ml/1 tsp sugar
10ml/2 tsp corn oil
2.5cm/1in cinnamon stick
2 black peppercorns
300ml/½ pint/1¼ cups water
115g/4oz panir, cubed
30ml/2 tbsp fresh coriander leaves
2 green chillies, seeded
  and chopped
50g/2oz fromage frais
75g/3oz frozen peas, thawed

peas *fromage frais* *chicken* *green chillies* *ground cardamom*
tomato purée *garam masala* *fresh coriander* *yogurt* *sugar* *garlic pulp* *chilli powder*
ginger pulp *panir* *salt* *ground turmeric* *peppercorns* *cinnamon stick*

COOK'S TIP
Panir is an Indian cheese made from whole milk and it provides a good source of protein.

1 Skin the chicken and cut it into 6–8 pieces.

2 Place the tomato purée, yogurt, garam masala, garlic pulp, ginger pulp, cardamom, chilli powder, turmeric, salt and sugar in a bowl and mix well.

3 Heat the oil with the whole spices in a non-stick wok or frying pan, then pour the sauce mixture into the oil. Lower the heat and cook for about 3 minutes, then pour in the water.

4 Add the chicken pieces and stir-fry for about 2 minutes, then cover and cook over a medium heat for about 10 minutes.

NUTRITIONAL NOTES
Per portion:

ENERGY 233 K Cals/977 K J **PROTEIN** 29.27g

FAT 10.28g **SATURATED FAT** 4.64g

CARBOHYDRATE 7.08g **FIBRE** 1.49g

ADDED SUGAR 1.06g

SALT 0.61g

5 Add the panir cubes to the pan, followed by half the coriander and half the green chillies. Stir to mix everything well and cook for a further 5–7 minutes.

6 Stir in the fromage frais and peas, heat through, then serve garnished with the remaining coriander and chillies.

Balti Chicken Vindaloo

This is considered rather a hot curry and is probably one of the best-known Indian dishes, especially in the West.

NUTRITIONAL NOTES
Per portion:
ENERGY 168 K Cals/704 K J **PROTEIN** 16.96g
FAT 4.20g **SATURATED FAT** 0.60g
CARBOHYDRATE 17.64g **FIBRE** 2.04g
ADDED SUGAR 0.01g
SALT 0.56g

Serves 4

INGREDIENTS
1 large potato
150ml/¼ pint/⅔ cup malt vinegar
7.5ml/1½ tsp crushed
  coriander seeds
5ml/1 tsp crushed cumin seeds
7.5ml/1½ tsp chilli powder
1.5ml/¼ tsp ground turmeric
5ml/1 tsp garlic pulp
5ml/1 tsp ginger pulp
5ml/1 tsp salt
7.5ml/1½ tsp paprika
15ml/1 tbsp tomato purée
large pinch of ground fenugreek
300ml/½ pint/1¼ cups water
225g/8oz boned and cubed
  skinless chicken breasts
15ml/1 tbsp corn oil
2 medium onions, sliced
4 curry leaves
2 green chillies, chopped

malt vinegar   potato   chicken breasts

chilli powder   onions   ginger pulp

paprika   green chillies   garlic pulp   salt

cumin seeds   curry leaves   coriander seeds

ground fenugreek   ground turmeric   tomato purée

1 Peel the potato, cut it into large, irregular shapes, place in a bowl of water and set aside.

2 Mix the vinegar with the coriander, cumin, chilli powder, turmeric, garlic, ginger, salt, paprika, tomato purée, fenugreek and water.

3 Pour this mixture over the chicken and set aside.

4 Heat the oil in a non-stick wok or frying pan and fry the onions with the curry leaves for 3–4 minutes.

COOK'S TIP
The best thing to drink with a hot curry is either iced water or a yogurt-based lassi.

5 Lower the heat and add the chicken mixture to the wok or frying pan. Continue to stir for a further 2 minutes. Drain the potato pieces and add to the pan. Cover with a lid and cook over a medium to low heat for 5–7 minutes or until the sauce has thickened slightly and the chicken and potatoes are cooked through.

6 Add the chopped green chillies before serving.

Balti Chicken Madras

This is a fairly hot chicken curry which is good served with either plain boiled rice, pilau rice or naan bread.

Serves 4

INGREDIENTS
275g/10oz boned, skinless
  chicken breasts
45ml/3 tbsp tomato purée
large pinch of ground fenugreek
1.5ml/¼ tsp ground fennel seeds
5ml/1 tsp ginger pulp
7.5ml/1½ tsp ground coriander
5ml/1 tsp garlic pulp
5ml/1 tsp chilli powder
1.5ml/¼ tsp ground turmeric
30ml/2 tbsp lemon juice
5ml/1 tsp salt
300ml/½ pint/1¼ cups water
15ml/1 tbsp corn oil
2 medium onions, diced
2–4 curry leaves
2 green chillies, seeded
  and chopped
15ml/1 tbsp fresh coriander leaves

chilli powder

onions

chicken breasts

lemon juice

green chillies

curry leaves

garlic pulp

tomato purée

fresh coriander

ground fennel

ground coriander

salt

ground fenugreek

ginger pulp

1 Cut the chicken breasts into bite-size cubes.

2 Place the tomato purée in a bowl with the fenugreek, fennel, ginger, ground coriander, garlic, chilli powder, turmeric, lemon juice, salt and water.

3 Heat the oil in a non-stick wok or frying pan and fry the onions together with the curry leaves until the onions are golden brown.

4 Add the chicken pieces to the onions and stir for about 1 minute to seal the meat.

5 Next pour in the sauce and continue to stir for about 2 minutes.

NUTRITIONAL NOTES

Per portion:

ENERGY 141 KCals/591 KJ **PROTEIN** 18.87g
FAT 4.11g **SATURATED FAT** 0.6g
CARBOHYDRATE 8.59g **FIBRE** 1.53g
ADDED SUGAR 0.01g
SALT 0.57g

COOK'S TIP
Always take care not to be over-generous when you are using ground fenugreek, as it can be quite bitter.

6 Lower the heat and cook for 8–10 minutes before adding the chillies and fresh coriander.

Balti Chicken in Hara Masala Sauce

This chicken can be served as an accompaniment to any of the rice dishes in this book.

Serves 4

INGREDIENTS
1 crisp green eating apple, peeled, cored and cut into small cubes
60ml/4 tbsp fresh coriander leaves
30ml/2 tbsp fresh mint leaves
120ml/4fl oz/½ cup natural low fat yogurt
45ml/3 tbsp fromage frais
2 medium green chillies, seeded and chopped
1 bunch spring onions, chopped
5ml/1 tsp salt
5ml/1 tsp sugar
5ml/1 tsp garlic pulp
5ml/1 tsp ginger pulp
15ml/1 tbsp corn oil
225g/8oz boned and cubed skinless chicken breasts
25g/1oz sultanas

apple

spring onions

chicken

sultanas

green chillies

fresh coriander

fromage frais

yogurt

garlic and ginger pulp

sugar

NUTRITIONAL NOTES
Per portion:
ENERGY 158 K Cals/666 K J **PROTEIN** 17.00g
FAT 4.37g **SATURATED FAT** 1.69g
CARBOHYDRATE 13.48g **FIBRE** 1.08g
ADDED SUGAR 1.06g **SALT** 0.56g

1 Place the apple, 45ml/3 tbsp of the coriander, the mint, yogurt, fromage frais, chillies, spring onions, salt, sugar, garlic and ginger in a food processor and process for about 1 minute, using the pulsing action.

2 Heat the oil in a non-stick wok or frying pan, pour in the yogurt mixture and cook over a low heat for about 2 minutes.

3 Next add the chicken pieces and blend everything together. Cook over a medium/low heat for 12–15 minutes or until the chicken is fully cooked.

4 Finally, add the sultanas and remaining coriander before serving.

COOK'S TIP
This dish makes a good dinner-party centrepiece.

Balti Chicken in a Thick Creamy Coconut Sauce

If you like the flavour of coconut, you will really love this curry.

Serves 4

INGREDIENTS

15ml/1 tbsp ground almonds
15ml/1 tbsp desiccated coconut
85ml/3 fl oz/⅔ cup coconut milk
175g/6oz/⅔ cup fromage frais
7.5ml/1½ tsp ground coriander
5ml/1 tsp chilli powder
5ml/1 tsp garlic pulp
7.5ml/1½ tsp ginger pulp
5ml/1 tsp salt
15ml/1 tbsp corn oil
225g/8oz skinned chicken, cubed
3 green cardamom pods
1 bay leaf
1 dried red chilli, crushed
30ml/2 tbsp chopped
   fresh coriander

almonds
chilli powder
fresh coriander
chicken
garlic pulp
bay leaf
cardamom
red chilli
salt
coconut
fromage frais
coconut milk
ginger pulp
ground coriander

NUTRITIONAL NOTES
Per portion:

ENERGY 166 K Cals/696 K J PROTEIN 18.58g
FAT 8.30g SATURATED FAT 2.84g
CARBOHYDRATE 5.52g FIBRE 0.95g
ADDED SUGAR 0.86g
SALT 0.57g

1 Using a heavy-based saucepan, dry-roast the ground almonds and desiccated coconut until they turn a shade darker. Transfer to a mixing bowl.

2 Add the coconut milk, fromage frais, ground coriander, chilli powder, garlic, ginger and salt to a mixing bowl.

COOK'S TIP
Cut the chicken into small, equal-size cubes for quick and even cooking.

3 Heat the oil in a non-stick wok or frying pan and add the chicken cubes, cardamoms and bay leaf. Stir-fry for about 2 minutes to seal the chicken.

4 Pour in the coconut milk mixture and blend everything together. Lower the heat, add the chilli and fresh coriander, cover and cook for 10–12 minutes, stirring occasionally. Uncover, then stir and cook for a further 2 minutes before serving.

Balti Chicken Pieces with Cumin and Coriander Potatoes

NUTRITIONAL NOTES
Per portion:
ENERGY 2783 K Cals/1166 KJ PROTEIN 20.33g
FAT 10.76g SATURATED FAT 1.58g
CARBOHYDRATE 27.26g FIBRE 2.78g
ADDED SUGAR 0.17g
SALT 0.09g

The potatoes are cooked separately in the oven before being added to the chicken. Basmati Rice with Peas and Curry Leaves is a perfect accompaniment to this dish.

Serves 4

INGREDIENTS
150ml/¼ pint/⅔ cup natural low
    fat yogurt
25g/1oz ground almonds
7.5ml/1½ tsp ground coriander
2.5ml/½ tsp chilli powder
5ml/1 tsp garam masala
15ml/1 tbsp coconut milk
5ml/1 tsp garlic pulp
5ml/1 tsp ginger pulp
30ml/2 tbsp chopped
    fresh coriander
1 red chilli, seeded and chopped
225g/8 oz skinless chicken breasts,
    boned and cubed
15ml/1 tbsp corn oil
2 medium onions, sliced
3 green cardamom pods
2.5cm/1in cinnamon stick
2 cloves

FOR THE POTATOES
15ml/1 tbsp corn oil
8 baby potatoes, thickly sliced
1.5ml/¼ tsp cumin seeds
15ml/1 tbsp finely chopped
    fresh coriander

garlic pulp

baby potatoes

chilli powder

chicken

onions

red chilli

ground almonds

yogurt

fresh coriander

garam masala

cumin seeds

ginger pulp

ground coriander

coconut milk

cardamom

cloves

cinnamon stick

1 In a bowl mix together the yogurt, ground almonds, ground coriander, chilli powder, garam masala, coconut milk, garlic, ginger, half the fresh coriander and half the red chilli.

2 Place the chicken pieces in the mixture, mix well and leave to marinate for about 2 hours.

3 Meanwhile, for the potatoes, heat the oil in non-stick wok or frying pan. Add the potatoes, cumin seeds and fresh coriander and stir-fry for 2–3 minutes.

4 Transfer to a heatproof dish, cover and cook in a preheated oven at 180°C/350°F/Gas 4 for about 30 minutes or until the potatoes are cooked through.

5 When you are ready to cook the chicken, increase the oven temperature to 200°C/400°F/Gas 6. Heat the oil with the onions, cardamoms, cinnamon and cloves for about 1½ minutes.

COOK'S TIP
Fresh mint may also be added to the potatoes if you like them with a minty flavour.

6 Pour the chicken mixture into the onions and stir-fry for 5–7 minutes. Lower the heat, cover with a lid and cook for a further 5–7 minutes. Serve topped with the cooked potatoes and garnished with the remaining fresh coriander and red chilli.

Balti Chicken in a Spicy Lentil Sauce

Traditionally this dish is made with lamb, but it is equally delicious if chicken is substituted. The lentils are flavoured with a tarka, a seasoned oil, which is poured over them just before serving.

Serves 4

NUTRITIONAL NOTES
Per portion:
ENERGY 207 K Cals/868 K J PROTEIN 17.77g
FAT 7.07g SATURATED FAT 1.03g
CARBOHYDRATE 20.36g FIBRE 2.84g
ADDED SUGAR 0.01g
SALT 0.80g

INGREDIENTS
30ml/2 tbsp chana dhal
50g/2 oz/¼ cup masoor dhal
15ml/1 tbsp corn oil
2 medium onions, chopped
5ml/1 tsp garlic pulp
5ml/1 tsp ginger pulp
2.5ml/½ tsp ground turmeric
7.5ml/1½ tsp chilli powder
5ml/1 tsp garam masala
2.5ml/½ tsp ground coriander
7.5ml/1½ tsp salt
175g/6 oz skinless chicken breasts,
    boned and cubed
45ml/3 tbsp fresh coriander leaves
1–2 green chillies, seeded
    and chopped
30–45ml/2–3 tbsp lemon juice
300ml/½ pint/1¼ cups water
2 tomatoes, skinned and halved

FOR THE TARKA
5ml/1 tsp corn oil
2.5ml/½ tsp cumin seeds
2 garlic cloves
2 dried red chillies
4 curry leaves

curry leaves
onions
chicken
salt
tomatoes
fresh coriander
green chillies

chilli powder
ginger pulp
red chillies
garlic pulp
chana dhal
masoor dhal
cumin seeds
garlic
garam masala
lemon juice

1 Boil the chana dhal and masoor dhal together in a saucepan of water until soft and mushy. Set aside.

2 Heat the oil in a non-stick wok or frying pan and fry the onions until soft and golden brown. Stir in the garlic, ginger, turmeric, chilli powder, garam masala, ground coriander and salt.

3 Next add the chicken pieces and stir-fry for 5–7 minutes.

4 Add half the fresh coriander, the green chillies, lemon juice and water and cook for a further 3–5 minutes.

5 Pour in the chana dhal and masoor dhal, followed by the tomatoes. Add the remaining fresh coriander. Remove from the heat and set aside.

COOK'S TIP

If you want to make this a vegetarian dish, just replace the chicken with the same quantity of vegetables of your choice.

6 To make the tarka, heat the oil and add the cumin seeds, whole garlic cloves, dried chillies and curry leaves. Heat for about 30 seconds and, while it is still hot, pour it over the top of the dhal. Serve immediately.

Mini Mince Koftas in Onion Sauce

This kofta curry is very popular in most Indian homes. It is also extremely easy to make. Serve with pilau rice.

Serves 4

INGREDIENTS
225g/8oz lean minced lamb
10ml/2 tsp poppy seeds
1 medium onion, chopped
5ml/1 tsp ginger pulp
5ml/1 tsp garlic pulp
5ml/1 tsp salt
5ml/1 tsp chilli powder
7.5ml/1½ tsp ground coriander
30ml/2 tbsp fresh coriander leaves
1 small egg

FOR THE SAUCE
85ml/3 fl oz/⅔ cup natural low
   fat yogurt
30ml/2 tbsp tomato purée
5ml/1 tsp chilli powder
5ml/1 tsp salt
5ml/1 tsp garlic pulp
5ml/1 tsp ginger pulp
5ml/1 tsp garam masala
10ml/2 tsp corn oil
1 cinnamon bark
425ml/⅔ pint/1⅔ cups water

ground coriander   onion

garlic pulp   lamb

fresh coriander   poppy seeds

ginger pulp

salt   yogurt   garam masala   tomato purée   chilli powder

cinnamon bark

1 Place the lamb in a food processor and mince for about 1 minute. Remove from the processor, put in a bowl, tip the poppy seeds on top and set aside.

2 Place the onion in the food processor, together with the ginger pulp, garlic pulp, salt, chilli powder, ground coriander and half the fresh coriander. Grind this mixture for about 30 seconds, then blend it into the minced lamb.

3 Whisk the egg and thoroughly mix it into the minced lamb. Leave to stand for about 1 hour.

4 For the sauce, whisk together the yogurt, tomato purée, chilli powder, salt, garlic pulp, ginger pulp and garam masala.

5 Heat the oil with the cinnamon bark in a non-stick wok or frying pan for about 1 minute, then pour in the sauce. Lower the heat and cook for about 1 minute. Remove the wok or frying pan from the heat and set aside.

NUTRITIONAL NOTES
Per portion:
ENERGY 155 K Cals/647 K J   **PROTEIN** 14.74g
FAT 9.24g   **SATURATED FAT** 2.79g
CARBOHYDRATE 7.56g   **FIBRE** 1.16g
ADDED SUGAR 0
SALT 1.07g

COOK'S TIP
This curry is also absolutely delicious served with warm, freshly made chapatis.

6 Break off small balls of the mince mixture and make the koftas using your hands. When all the koftas are ready, return the sauce to the heat and add the water. Drop in the koftas one by one. Place the remaining fresh coriander on top, cover with a lid and cook for 7–10 minutes, stirring gently occasionally to turn the koftas around. Serve hot.

Spiced Lamb with Chillies

This is a fairly hot stir-fry dish, although you can, of course, make it less so by reducing the quantity of chillies.

NUTRITIONAL NOTES
Per portion:
ENERGY 169 K Cals/706 K J PROTEIN 14.95g
FAT 8.13g SATURATED FAT 2.71g
CARBOHYDRATE 10.00g FIBRE 1.32g
ADDED SUGAR 0.01g
SALT 0.57g

Serves 4

INGREDIENTS
225g/8oz lean lamb fillet
120ml/4fl oz/½ cup natural low
    fat yogurt
1.5ml/¼ tsp ground cardamom
5ml/1 tsp ginger pulp
5ml/1 tsp garlic pulp
5ml/1 tsp chilli powder
5ml/1 tsp garam masala
5ml/1 tsp salt
15ml/1 tbsp corn oil
2 medium onions, chopped
1 bay leaf
300ml/½ pint/1¼ cups water
2 red chillies, seeded and
    sliced lengthways
2 green chillies, seeded and
    sliced lengthways
30ml/2 tbsp fresh coriander leaves

onions

lamb fillet

garlic pulp

ginger pulp

bay leaf

red and green chillies

 salt

fresh coriander

 yogurt

 cardamom

chilli powder

garam masala

1 Using a sharp knife, cut the lamb into even-size strips.

2 Mix together the yogurt, cardamom, ginger pulp, garlic pulp, chilli powder, garam masala and salt. Add the lamb and leave for about 1 hour to marinate.

3 Heat the oil in a non-stick wok or frying pan and fry the onions 3–5 minutes, or until golden brown.

4 Add the bay leaf, then add the lamb with the yogurt and spices and stir-fry for 2–3 minutes over a medium heat.

5 Pour over the water, cover and cook for 15–20 minutes over a low heat, checking occasionally. Once the water has evaporated, stir-fry the mixture for 1 further minute.

6 Add the red and green chillies and the fresh coriander and serve hot.

Balti Lamb with Peas and Potatoes

Fresh mint leaves are used in this dish, but if they are obtainable, use ready-minted frozen peas to bring an added freshness. Serve with rice.

Serves 4

INGREDIENTS
225g/8oz lean spring lamb
120ml/4 fl oz/½ cup natural low
   fat yogurt
1 cinnamon stick
2 green cardamom pods
3 black peppercorns
5ml/1 tsp garlic pulp
5ml/1 tsp ginger pulp
5ml/1 tsp chilli powder
5ml/1 tsp garam masala
5ml/1 tsp salt
30ml/2 tbsp roughly chopped
   fresh mint
15ml/3 tbsp corn oil
2 medium onions, sliced
300ml/½ pint/1¼ cups water
115g/4oz frozen peas
1 large potato, diced
1 firm tomato, skinned, seeded
   and diced

garlic pulp *potato*

lamb

garam masala *onions* *salt*

cardamom peppercorns *cinnamon stick*

ginger pulp

mint

peas

chilli powder *tomato* *yogurt*

1 Using a sharp knife, cut the lamb into strips, then place it in a bowl.

2 Add the yogurt, cinnamon, cardamoms, peppercorns, garlic, ginger, chilli powder, garam masala, salt and half the mint. Leave to marinate for about 2 hours.

3 Heat the oil in a non-stick wok or frying pan and fry the onions until golden brown. Stir in the lamb and the marinade and stir-fry for about 3 minutes.

4 Pour in the water, lower the heat and cook until the meat is cooked right through, about 15 minutes, depending on the age of the lamb. Meanwhile cook the potato in boiling water until just soft, but not mushy.

5 Add the peas and potato to the lamb and stir to mix gently.

NUTRITIONAL NOTES
Per portion:

ENERGY 231 K Cals/968 K J **PROTEIN** 17.54g
FAT 8.47g **SATURATED FAT** 2.79g
CARBOHYDRATE 22.72g **FIBRE** 3.73g
ADDED SUGAR 0
SALT 0.57g

COOK'S TIP
You can cook this dish in advance and keep it in the fridge. In fact, this will improve the flavour.

6 Finally, add the remaining mint and the tomato and cook for a further 5 minutes before serving.

Balti Spring Lamb Chops

It is best to marinate the chops overnight as this makes them very tender and also helps them to absorb the maximum amount of flavour. Serve with a crisp salad.

Serves 4

INGREDIENTS
8 small lean spring lamb chops
1 large red chilli, seeded
30ml/2 tbsp chopped fresh
    coriander
15ml/1 tbsp chopped fresh mint
5ml/1 tsp salt
5ml/1 tsp soft brown sugar
5ml/1 tsp garam masala
5ml/1 tsp garlic pulp
5ml/1 tsp ginger pulp
175ml/6 fl oz/⅔ cup natural low
    fat yogurt
10ml/2 tsp corn oil

garlic pulp

garam masala

lamb chops

ginger pulp

mint

fresh coriander

salt

red chilli

yogurt

brown sugar

NUTRITIONAL NOTES
Per portion:
ENERGY 207 K Cals/864 K J **PROTEIN** 23.15g
FAT 10.29g **SATURATED FAT** 4.26g
CARBOHYDRATE 5.62g **FIBRE** 0.27g
ADDED SUGAR 1.01g
SALT 0.6g

1 Trim the lamb chops to remove any excess fat. Place them in a large bowl.

2 Finely chop the chilli, then mix with the coriander, mint, salt, brown sugar, garam masala, garlic pulp and ginger pulp.

COOK'S TIP
These chops can also be grilled. Remember to baste with oil.

3 Pour the yogurt into the herb mixture and, using a small whisk or a fork, mix thoroughly. Pour this mixture over the top of the chops and turn them with your fingers to make sure that they are completely covered. Leave to marinate overnight in the fridge.

4 Heat the oil in a large, non-stick wok or frying pan and add the chops. Lower the heat and allow to cook over a medium heat. Turn the chops over and continue frying until they are cooked right through – about 20 minutes – turning again if needed.

Creamy Lamb Korma

Cutting the lamb into strips for this lovely dish makes it easier and quicker to cook.

Serves 4

INGREDIENTS
2 green chillies, seeded
120ml/4 fl oz/½ cup natural low
   fat yogurt
50ml/2 fl oz/¼ cup coconut milk
15ml/1 tbsp ground almonds
5ml/1 tsp salt
5ml/1 tsp garlic pulp
5ml/1 tsp ginger pulp
5ml/1 tsp garam masala
1.5ml/¼ tsp ground cardamom
large pinch of ground cinnamon
15ml/1 tbsp chopped fresh mint
15ml/1 tbsp corn oil
2 medium onions, diced
1 bay leaf
4 black peppercorns
225g/8oz lean lamb, cut into strips
150ml/¼ pint/⅔ cup water
mint leaves, to garnish

almonds
onions
lamb
peppercorns
cinnamon   mint   bay leaf
ground cardamom   coconut milk   green chillies
garam masala   garlic pulp   ginger pulp   yogurt

NUTRITIONAL NOTES
Per portion:
ENERGY 193 K Cals/803 K J PROTEIN 15.50g
FAT 10.14g SATURATED FAT 2.91g
CARBOHYDRATE 10.47g FIBRE 1.60g
ADDED SUGAR 0.58g SALT 0.58g

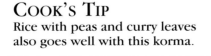

1 Finely chop the chillies. Whisk the yogurt with the chillies, coconut milk, ground almonds, salt, garlic, ginger, garam masala, cardamom, cinnamon and mint.

2 Heat the oil in a non-stick wok or frying pan and fry the onions with the bay leaf and peppercorns.

COOK'S TIP
Rice with peas and curry leaves also goes well with this korma.

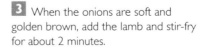

3 When the onions are soft and golden brown, add the lamb and stir-fry for about 2 minutes.

4 Pour in the yogurt mixture and water, lower the heat, cover and cook for about 15 minutes or until the lamb is cooked through, stirring occasionally. Stir-fry for a further 2 minutes. Serve garnished with mint leaves.

Balti Lamb in a Yogurt and Garam Masala Sauce

The lamb is first marinated and then cooked slowly in a hot yogurt sauce. It is served with dried apricots that have been lightly sautéed in a low fat spread with cinnamon and cardamom.

Serves 4

INGREDIENTS
15ml/1 tbsp tomato purée
175ml/6 fl oz/⅔ cup natural low
    fat yogurt
5ml/1 tsp garam masala
1.5ml/¼ tsp cumin seeds
5ml/1 tsp salt
5ml/1 tsp garlic pulp
5ml/1 tsp ginger pulp
5ml/1 tsp chilli powder
225g/8oz lean spring lamb, cut
    into strips
15ml/3 tsp corn oil
2 medium onions, finely sliced
25g/1oz low fat spread
2.5cm/1in cinnamon stick
2 green cardamom pods
5 dried apricots, quartered
15ml/1 tbsp fresh coriander leaves

garam masala   onions   lamb
chilli powder   salt   yogurt
coriander
tomato purée   ginger pulp   cinnamon stick
cardamom
cumin seeds   apricots
garlic pulp

1 In a bowl, blend together the tomato purée, yogurt, garam masala, cumin seeds, salt, garlic, ginger and chilli powder. Place the lamb in the sauce and leave to marinate for about 1 hour.

2 Heat 10ml/2 tsp of the oil in a non-stick wok or frying pan and fry the onions until crisp and golden brown.

3 Remove the onions using a slotted spoon, allow to cool and then grind down by processing briefly in a food processor or with a pestle in a mortar. Reheat the remaining oil and return the onions to the wok.

4 Add the lamb and stir-fry for about 2 minutes. Cover, lower the heat and cook, stirring occasionally, for 15 minutes or until the meat is cooked through. If required, add about 150ml/¼ pint/⅔ cup water during the cooking. Remove from the heat and set aside.

5 Heat the low fat spread with the remaining oil and drop in the cinnamon stick and cardamoms. Add the dried apricots and stir over a low heat for about 2 minutes. Pour this over the lamb.

NUTRITIONAL NOTES

Per portion:

ENERGY 215 K Cals/896 K J **PROTEIN** 16.24g
FAT 10.32g **SATURATED FAT** 3.41g
CARBOHYDRATE 15.51g **FIBRE** 2.25g
ADDED SUGAR 1.26g
SALT 0.64g

COOK'S TIP

If you want this curry to be slightly hotter, increase the garam masala and chilli powder to 7.5ml/1½ tsp each.

6 Serve garnished with the coriander.

Balti Bhoona Lamb

Bhoona is a very traditional way of stir-frying which simply involves semi-circular movements, scraping the bottom of the wok each time in the centre. Serve with a freshly-made chapati.

Serves 4

INGREDIENTS
225–275g/8–10oz boned lean
   spring lamb
3 medium onions
15ml/1 tbsp olive oil
15ml/1 tbsp tomato purée
5ml/1 tsp garlic pulp
7.5ml/1½ tsp ginger pulp
5ml/1 tsp salt
1.5ml/¼ tsp ground turmeric
600ml/1 pint/2½ cups water
15ml/1 tbsp lemon juice
15ml/1 tbsp shredded fresh
   root ginger
15ml/1 tbsp chopped
   fresh coriander
15ml/1 tbsp chopped fresh mint
1 red chilli, seeded and chopped

red chilli
onions
tomato purée • salt
lamb
mint • fresh coriander
ground turmeric • garlic pulp
ginger pulp • ginger • lemon juice

NUTRITIONAL NOTES
Per portion:
ENERGY 198 K Cals/825 KJ **PROTEIN** 16.07g
FAT 10.37g **SATURATED FAT** 3.24g
CARBOHYDRATE 11.05g **FIBRE** 1.84g
ADDED SUGAR 0
SALT 0.56g

1 Using a sharp knife, cut the lamb into small cubes.

2 Dice the onions finely. Heat the oil in a non-stick wok or frying pan and fry the onions until soft.

3 Meanwhile, mix together the tomato purée, garlic, ginger, salt and turmeric. Pour the spice mixture into the wok and briefly stir-fry.

4 Add the lamb and continue to stir-fry for about 2–3 minutes. Stir in the water, lower the heat, cover and cook for 15–20 minutes, stirring occasionally.

5 When the water has almost evaporated, start bhooning over a medium heat (see the introduction above), making sure that the sauce does not catch on the bottom of the wok. Continue for 5–7 minutes.

6 Pour in the lemon juice, followed by the ginger, coriander, mint and red chilli, then serve.

Balti Lamb with Cauliflower

Cauliflower and lamb go beautifully together. This curry is given a final tarka of cumin seeds and curry leaves, which enhances the flavour.

Serves 4

INGREDIENTS

10ml/2 tsp corn oil
2 medium onions, sliced
7.5ml/1½ tsp ginger pulp
5ml/1 tsp chilli powder
5ml/1 tsp garlic pulp
1.5ml/¼ tsp ground turmeric
2.5ml/½ tsp ground coriander
30ml/2 tbsp fresh fenugreek leaves
275g/10oz boned lean spring lamb,
    cut into strips
1 small cauliflower, cut into
    small florets
300ml/½ pint/1¼ cups water
30ml/2 tbsp fresh coriander leaves
½ red pepper, seeded and sliced
15ml/1 tbsp lemon juice

FOR THE TARKA

10ml/2 tsp corn oil
2.5ml/½ tsp white cumin seeds
4–6 curry leaves

1 Heat the oil in a non-stick wok or frying pan and fry the onions until golden brown. Lower the heat and add the ginger pulp, chilli powder, garlic pulp, turmeric and ground coriander, followed by the fenugreek.

2 Add the lamb strips to the wok and stir-fry until the lamb is completely coated with the spices. Add half the cauliflower florets and stir the mixture well.

ground coriander

lamb

cumin seeds

curry leaves

lemon juice

fenugreek

cauliflower

fresh coriander

onions

red pepper

ground turmeric

chilli powder

ginger pulp

garlic pulp

COOK'S TIP

If you wish, you may use a good-quality olive oil for the tarka.

3 Pour in the water, cover the wok, lower the heat and cook for 5–7 minutes until the cauliflower and lamb are almost cooked through.

4 Add the remaining cauliflower, half the fresh coriander, the red pepper and lemon juice and stir-fry for about 5 minutes, making sure that the sauce does not catch on the bottom of the wok.

NUTRITIONAL NOTES

Per portion:

ENERGY 202 K Cals/839 K J **PROTEIN** 18.42g
FAT 9.88g **SATURATED FAT** 3.24g
CARBOHYDRATE 10.86g **FIBRE** 2.88g
ADDED SUGAR 0
SALT 0.07g

5 Check that the lamb is completely cooked, then remove from the heat and set aside.

6 To make the tarka, heat the oil and fry the seeds and curry leaves for about 30 seconds. While it is still hot, pour the seasoned oil over the cauliflower and lamb and serve garnished with the remaining fresh coriander leaves.

Balti Masala Keema

A rather spicy keema, as the name suggests. You could add a vegetable of your choice to this if you wish. Serve with rice or chapatis.

Serves 4

INGREDIENTS
15ml/1 tbsp corn oil
2 cardamom pods
2.5cm/1in cinnamon stick
2 cloves
3 black peppercorns
3 medium onions, chopped
350g/12oz lean minced lamb
7.5ml/1½ tsp garam masala
5ml/1 tsp chilli powder
5ml/1 tsp garlic pulp
7.5ml/1½ tsp ginger pulp
5ml/1 tsp salt
1 large potato, cut into small cubes
2 tomatoes, skinned and diced
30ml/2 tbsp fresh coriander leaves

onions

salt

tomatoes

lamb

fresh coriander

cloves   cardamom
peppercorns

cinnamon stick

garam masala

ginger pulp   garlic pulp   potato   chilli powder

NUTRITIONAL NOTES
Per portion:
ENERGY 241 K Cals/1007 K J PROTEIN 20.75g
FAT 9.33g SATURATED FAT 3.55g
CARBOHYDRATE 19.87g FIBRE 2.63g
ADDED SUGAR 0
SALT 0.57g

1 Heat the oil in a non-stick wok or frying pan and fry the whole spices for about 1 minute. Add the onions and continue to fry for a further 3 minutes.

2 Meanwhile put the lamb into a bowl and mix in the garam masala, chilli powder, garlic, ginger and salt.

3 Tip the lamb mixture into the frying onions and stir-fry for 5–7 minutes.

4 Add the potato and tomato. Chop half the coriander leaves and add these. Cover the wok and cook over a low heat for 3–5 minutes so that the potato is cooked in the steam. Garnish with the remaining coriander leaves and serve.

Balti Keema with Curry Leaves and Green Chillies

Minced lamb is cooked in its own juices with a few spices and herbs, but no other liquid.

Serves 4

INGREDIENTS
10ml/2 tsp corn oil
2 medium onions, chopped
10 curry leaves
6 green chillies
350g/12oz lean minced lamb
5ml/1 tsp garlic pulp
5ml/1 tsp ginger pulp
5ml/1 tsp chilli powder
1.5ml/¼ tsp ground turmeric
5ml/1 tsp salt
2 tomatoes, skinned and quartered
15ml/1 tbsp chopped
    fresh coriander

onions

chilli powder

lamb

curry leaves

ground turmeric   green chillies   salt

ginger pulp   tomatoes   fresh coriander   garlic pulp

NUTRITIONAL NOTES
Per portion:
ENERGY 197 K Cals/821 K J PROTEIN 20.25g
FAT 9.37g SATURATED FAT 3.59g
CARBOHYDRATE 8.54g FIBRE 1.63g
ADDED SUGAR 0.03g
SALT 0.57g

1 Heat the oil in a non-stick wok or frying pan and fry the onions together with the curry leaves and 3 of the whole green chillies.

2 Put the lamb into a bowl and add the garlic, ginger, chilli powder, turmeric and salt. Blend everything thoroughly.

COOK'S TIP
This curry also make a terrific brunch if served with fried eggs.

3 Tip the lamb mixture into the onions and stir-fry for 7–10 minutes, lowering the heat to medium if necessary.

4 Add the tomatoes and coriander and the remaining whole green chillies. Continue to stir-fry for a further 2 minutes before serving.

Courgettes with Lamb

Lamb is cooked with yogurt and then the courgettes, which have already been grilled, are added to the mixture.

Serves 4

INGREDIENTS
15ml/1 tbsp corn oil
2 medium onions, chopped
225g/8oz lean lamb steaks, cut into strips
120ml/4 fl oz/½ cup natural low fat yogurt
5ml/1 tsp garam masala
5ml/1 tsp chilli powder
5ml/1 tsp garlic pulp
5ml/1 tsp ginger pulp
2.5ml/½ tsp ground coriander
2 medium courgettes, sliced
15ml/1 tbsp chopped fresh coriander, to garnish

onions

courgettes

lamb

garlic pulp

ginger pulp

fresh coriander

chilli powder

ground coriander

garam masala

yogurt

NUTRITIONAL NOTES
Per portion:
ENERGY 178 K Cals/742 K J PROTEIN 15.80g
FAT 8.36g SATURATED FAT 2.78g
CARBOHYDRATE 10.83g FIBRE 1.99g
ADDED SUGAR 0
SALT 0.08g

1 Heat the oil in a non-stick wok or frying pan and fry the onions until they are golden brown.

2 Add the lamb strips and stir-fry for 1 minute to seal the meat.

3 Put the yogurt, garam masala, chilli powder, garlic, ginger and ground coriander into a bowl. Whisk the mixture together.

4 Pour the yogurt mixture over the lamb and stir-fry for a further 2 minutes. Cover and cook over a medium to low heat for 12–15 minutes.

5 Put the courgettes in a flameproof dish and cook on a preheated grill for about 3 minutes, turning once.

6 Check that the lamb is cooked through and the sauce is quite thick, then add the courgettes and serve garnished with the fresh coriander.

Stir-fried Lamb with Baby Onions and Peppers

The baby onions are used whole in this recipe.
Serve with rice or lentils.

NUTRITIONAL NOTES
Per portion:
ENERGY 155 K Cals/644 K J PROTEIN 12.75g
FAT 9.48g SATURATED FAT 2.82g
CARBOHYDRATE 5.74g FIBRE 1.49g
ADDED SUGAR 0
SALT 0.55g

Serves 4

INGREDIENTS
15ml/1 tbsp corn oil
8 baby onions
225g/8oz boned lean lamb, cut
  into strips
5ml/1 tsp ground cumin
5ml/1 tsp ground coriander
15ml/1 tbsp tomato purée
5ml/1 tsp chilli powder
5ml/1 tsp salt
15ml/1 tbsp lemon juice
2.5ml/½ tsp onion seeds
4 curry leaves
300ml/½ pint/1¼ cups water
1 small red pepper, seeded and
  roughly sliced
1 small green pepper, seeded and
  roughly sliced
15ml/1 tbsp chopped
  fresh coriander
15ml/1 tbsp chopped fresh mint

onions

green and
red peppers   lamb

onion
seeds

lemon juice

mint   curry
       leaves

fresh
coriander

ground cumin   ground
                coriander   chilli
                             powder

tomato purée   salt

1 Heat the oil in a non-stick wok or frying pan and stir-fry the whole baby onions for about 3 minutes. Using a slotted spoon, remove the onions from the wok and set aside to drain.

2 Mix together the lamb, cumin, ground coriander, tomato purée, chilli powder, salt and lemon juice in a bowl and set aside.

3 Reheat the oil and stir-fry the onion seeds and curry leaves for 2–3 minutes.

4 Add the lamb and spice mixture and stir-fry for about 5 minutes, then pour in the water, lower the heat and cook gently for about 10 minutes, until the lamb is cooked through.

5 Add the peppers and half the fresh coriander and mint. Stir-fry for a further 2 minutes.

6 Finally, add the baby onions and the remaining fresh coriander and chopped mint and serve.

COOK'S TIP
This dish benefits from being cooked a day in advance and kept in the fridge .

Basmati Rice with Prawns and Vegetables

This is an excellent combination of prawns and vegetables, which is lightly flavoured with whole spices. Using frozen mixed vegetables speeds up the preparation time. Serve with raita.

Serves 4

INGREDIENTS
300g/11oz basmati rice
15ml/1 tbsp corn oil
2 medium onions, sliced
3 green cardamom pods
2.5cm/1in cinnamon stick
4 black peppercorns
1 bay leaf
1.5ml/¼ tsp black cumin seeds
5ml/1 tsp shredded fresh
    root ginger
2 garlic cloves, roughly chopped
2 green chillies, seeded
    and chopped
30ml/2 tbsp chopped
    fresh coriander
30ml/2 tbsp lemon juice
115g/4oz frozen mixed vegetables
    (carrots, beans, sweetcorn
    and peas)
175–225g/6–8oz frozen cooked
    peeled prawns, thawed
500ml/16 fl oz/2 cups water

1 Wash the rice well and leave it to soak in water.

onions
prawns
bay leaf
garlic
cinnamon stick
green chillies
fresh coriander
lemon juice
cumin seeds
ginger
peppercorns
cardamom
basmati rice
mixed vegetables

2 Heat the oil in a heavy-based saucepan and fry the onions, cardamoms, cinnamon stick, peppercorns, bay leaf, cumin seeds, ginger, garlic and chillies for about 3 minutes.

3 Add half the fresh coriander, the lemon juice, the mixed vegetables and the prawns. Stir for a further 3 minutes.

4 Drain the rice and add it to the pan. Gently stir in the water and bring to the boil. Lower the heat, add the remaining fresh coriander and cook, covered with a lid, for 15–20 minutes or until all the liquid has been absorbed and the rice is cooked through. Allow to stand, still covered, for 5–7 minutes before serving.

COOK'S TIP
This makes a very impressive dinner party dish and looks attractive decorated with large prawns in their shells.

<u>NUTRITIONAL NOTES</u>
Per portion:
ENERGY 410 K Cals/1737 K J **PROTEIN** 20.52g
FAT 6.33g **SATURATED FAT** 1.13g
CARBOHYDRATE 72.32g **FIBRE** 1.37g
ADDED SUGAR 0.01g
SALT 0.93g

Basmati Rice with Peas and Curry Leaves

A very simple rice dish, full of flavour.

Serves 4

INGREDIENTS
300g/11oz basmati rice
15ml/1 tbsp corn oil
6–8 curry leaves
1.5ml/¼ tsp mustard seeds
1.5ml/¼ tsp onion seeds
30ml/2 tbsp fresh fenugreek leaves
5ml/1 tsp garlic pulp
5ml/1 tsp ginger pulp
5ml/1 tsp salt
115g/4oz frozen peas
500ml/16fl oz/2 cups water

garlic pulp   peas   basmati rice

mustard seeds   fenugreek   curry leaves

salt   ginger pulp   onion seeds

NUTRITIONAL NOTES
Per portion:
ENERGY 336 K Cals/1425 K J **PROTEIN** 7.79g
FAT 5.96g **SATURATED FAT** 1.09g
CARBOHYDRATE 67.67g **FIBRE** 1.83g
ADDED SUGAR 0
SALT 0.49g

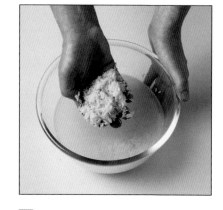

1 Wash the rice well and leave it to soak in water.

2 Heat the oil in a heavy-based saucepan with the curry leaves, mustard seeds, onion seeds, fenugreek, garlic pulp, ginger pulp and salt and stir-fry for 2–3 minutes.

COOK'S TIP
Curry leaves freeze very well, so it is worth keeping a stock in the freezer.

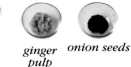

3 Drain the rice, add it to the pan and stir gently.

4 Add the frozen peas and water and bring to the boil. Lower the heat, cover with a lid and cook for 15–20 minutes. Remove from the heat and leave to stand, still covered, for 10 minutes before serving.

Basmati Rice with Potatoes

Rice is eaten at all meals in Indian and Pakistani homes. There are several ways of cooking rice and mostly whole spices are used. Always choose a good-quality basmati rice.

Serves 4

INGREDIENTS
300g/11oz basmati rice
15ml/1 tbsp corn oil
1 cinnamon bark
1 bay leaf
1.5ml/¼ tsp black cumin seeds
3 green cardamom pods
1 medium onion, sliced
5ml/1 tsp ginger pulp
5ml/1 tsp garlic pulp
1.5ml/¼ tsp ground turmeric
7.5ml/1½ tsp salt
1 large potato, roughly diced
500ml/16fl oz/2 cups water
15ml/1 tbsp chopped
    fresh coriander

cumin seeds   potato   basmati rice

ginger pulp   ground turmeric   cardamom   cinnamon bark

onion   bay leaf

salt   fresh coriander   garlic pulp

NUTRITIONAL NOTES
Per portion:
ENERGY 371 K Cals/1572 KJ PROTEIN 7.43g
FAT 5.72g SATURATED FAT 1.03g
CARBOHYDRATE 77.36g FIBRE 1.62g
ADDED SUGAR 0 SALT 0.75g

1 Wash the rice well and leave it to soak in water. Heat the oil in a heavy-based saucepan, add the cinnamon, bay leaf, cumin seeds, cardamoms and onion and cook for about 2 minutes.

2 Add the ginger, garlic, turmeric, salt and potato and continue to cook for about 1 minute.

COOK'S TIP
Serve the rice using a slotted spoon and handle it gently.

3 Drain the rice and add it to the pan.

4 Stir to mix, then pour in the water followed by the coriander. Cover the pan with a lid and cook for 15–20 minutes. Remove from the heat and leave to stand, still covered, for 5–10 minutes before serving.

Rice with Mushrooms and Prawns

Although mushrooms are not a very common vegetable in India, this dish provides a perfect combination of flavours.

Serves 4

INGREDIENTS
150g/5oz basmati rice
15ml/1 tbsp corn oil
1 medium onion, chopped
4 black peppercorns
2.5cm/1in cinnamon stick
1 bay leaf
1.5ml/¼ tsp black cumin seeds
2 cardamom pods
5ml/1 tsp garlic pulp
5ml/1 tsp ginger pulp
5ml/1 tsp garam masala
5ml/1 tsp chilli powder
7.5ml/1½ tsp salt
115g/4oz frozen cooked, peeled
    prawns, thawed
115g/4oz mushrooms, cut into
    large pieces
30ml/2 tbsp chopped
    fresh coriander
120ml/4fl oz/½ cup natural
    low fat yogurt
15ml/1 tbsp lemon juice
50g/2oz frozen peas
250ml/8fl oz/1 cup water
1 red chilli, seeded and sliced,
    to garnish

basmati rice   *mushrooms*   *prawns*

chilli powder   *garam masala*   *onion*   *salt*

yogurt   *peppercorns*   *cinnamon stick*   *cardamom*   *bay leaf*

ginger pulp   *cumin seeds*   *red chilli*

garlic pulp   *lemon juice*   *peas*   *fresh coriander*

1 Wash the rice well and leave to soak in water.

2 Heat the oil in a non-stick wok or frying pan and add the onion, peppercorns, cinnamon, bay leaf, cumin seeds, cardamoms, garlic pulp, ginger pulp, garam masala, chilli powder and salt. Lower the heat and stir-fry for about 2 minutes.

3 Add the prawns and cook for 2 minutes, before adding the mushrooms.

4 Add the coriander and the yogurt, followed by the lemon juice and peas.

NUTRITIONAL NOTES

Per portion:

ENERGY 248 K Cals/1050 K J **PROTEIN** 13.12g
FAT 5.20g **SATURATED FAT** 0.99g
CARBOHYDRATE 40.04g **FIBRE** 1.85g
ADDED SUGAR 0
SALT 1.23g

5 Drain the rice and add it to the prawn mixture. Pour in the water, cover the pan and cook over a medium heat for about 15 minutes, checking once.

6 Remove from the heat and leave to stand, still covered, for about 5 minutes. Transfer to a serving dish and serve garnished with the sliced red chilli.

Fried Sesame Seed Chutney

This is a versatile chutney, which doubles as a delicious dip, served with poppadoms, and also makes a tasty sandwich filling with cucumber.

Serves 4

INGREDIENTS
175g/6oz sesame seeds
5ml/1 tsp salt
120–150ml/4–5fl oz/½–⅔ cup water
2 green chillies, seeded and diced
60ml/4 tbsp chopped
  fresh coriander
15ml/1 tbsp chopped fresh mint
15ml/1 tbsp tamarind paste
30ml/2 tbsp sugar
5ml/1 tsp corn oil
1.5ml/¼ tsp onion seeds
4 curry leaves
6 onion rings, 1 green chilli, seeded
  and sliced, 1 red chilli, seeded and
  sliced, 15ml/1 tbsp fresh coriander
  leaves, to garnish

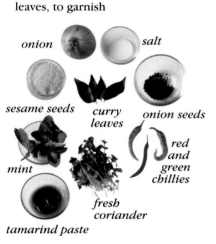

onion   salt

sesame seeds   curry   onion seeds
             leaves
                            red
                            and
                            green
mint   chillies

        fresh
        coriander

tamarind paste

NUTRITIONAL NOTES

Per portion:

ENERGY 347 K Cals/1438 K J   PROTEIN 8.94g
FAT 28.31g   SATURATED FAT 4.03g
CARBOHYDRATE 14.80g   FIBRE 3.63g
ADDED SUGAR 10.51g
SALT 0.5g

1 Dry-roast the sesame seeds and leave to cool. Place them in a spice grinder and grind to a grainy powder.

2 Transfer the sesame powder to a bowl. Add the salt, water, diced chillies, coriander, mint, tamarind paste and sugar and, using a fork, mix everything together. Taste and adjust the seasoning if necessary: the mixture should have a sweet-and-sour flavour.

3 Heat the oil in a heavy-based saucepan and fry the onion seeds and curry leaves. Tip the sesame seed paste into the pan and stir-fry for about 45 seconds. Transfer to a serving dish.

4 Garnish with onion rings, sliced green and red chillies and the coriander.

Sweet-and-sour Raita

Raitas are traditionally served with most meals as accompaniments that are cooling to the palate. Raitas are also served with Biryanis.

Serves 4

INGREDIENTS
500ml/16fl oz/2 cups natural
   low fat yogurt
5ml/1 tsp salt
5ml/1 tsp sugar
30ml/2 tbsp honey
7.5ml/1½ tsp mint sauce
30ml/2 tbsp roughly chopped
   fresh coriander
1 green chilli, seeded and
   finely chopped
1 medium onion, diced
50ml/2fl oz/¼ cup water

onion *yogurt*

mint sauce *fresh coriander* *green chilli*

honey *sugar*

NUTRITIONAL NOTES
Per portion:
ENERGY 128 K Cals/541 K J **PROTEIN** 7.42g
FAT 1.18g **SATURATED FAT** 0.64g
CARBOHYDRATE 23.34g **FIBRE** 0.53g
ADDED SUGAR 1.06g
SALT 0.62g

1 Pour the yogurt into a bowl and whisk it well. Add the salt, sugar, honey and mint sauce.

2 Reserve a little coriander for the garnish and add the rest to the yogurt mixture, with the chilli, onion and water.

COOK'S TIP
Peeled cucumber can also be used for this recipe.

3 Taste to check the sweetness and add more honey, if desired.

4 Whisk once again and pour into a serving bowl. Garnish with the reserved coriander and place in the fridge until ready to serve.

Tomato and Onion Chutney

Chutneys are served with most meat dishes in Indian cuisine.

Serves 4

INGREDIENTS
8 tomatoes
1 medium onion, chopped
45ml/3 tbsp brown sugar
5ml/1 tsp garam masala
5ml/1 tsp ginger powder
175ml/6fl oz/⅔ cup malt vinegar
5ml/1 tsp salt
15ml/1 tbsp clear honey
natural low fat yogurt, sliced green
   chilli and fresh mint leaves,
   to garnish

onions   *malt vinegar*
brown sugar
mint
honey
tomatoes
garam masala
ginger powder
yogurt

NUTRITIONAL NOTES

Per portion:
ENERGY 118 K Cals/503 K J   PROTEIN 1.94g
FAT 0.66g   SATURATED FAT 0.18g
CARBOHYDRATE 28.70g   FIBRE 2.34g
ADDED SUGAR 15.20g
SALT 0.52g

1 Wash the tomatoes and cut them into quarters.

2 Place them with the onion in a heavy-based saucepan.

COOK'S TIP
This chutney will keep for about 2 weeks in a covered jar in the fridge.

3 Add the sugar, garam masala, ginger, vinegar, salt and honey, half-cover the pan with a lid and cook over a low heat for about 20 minutes.

4 Mash the tomatoes with a fork to break them up, then continue to cook on a slightly higher heat until the chutney thickens. Serve chilled, garnished with yogurt, sliced chilli and mint leaves.

Sweet-and-sour Tomato and Onion Relish

A delicious and quick relish that can be served with any meal.

Serves 4

INGREDIENTS
2 medium firm tomatoes
1 medium onion
1 green chilli
15ml/1 tbsp fresh mint leaves
15ml/1 tbsp fresh coriander leaves
2.5ml/½ tsp Tabasco sauce
15ml/1 tbsp clear honey
2.5ml/½ tsp salt
30ml/2 tbsp lime juice
15ml/1 tbsp natural low fat yogurt

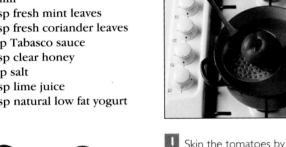

tomatoes   *onion*

honey   *green chilli*

lime juice   *mint*   *coriander*

salt   *Tabasco sauce*   *yogurt*

NUTRITIONAL NOTES
Per portion:
ENERGY 43 K Cals/180 K J   PROTEIN 1.22g
FAT 0.29g   SATURATED FAT 0.06g
CARBOHYDRATE 9.39g   FIBRE 0.96g
ADDED SUGAR 0.04g
SALT 0.26g

1 Skin the tomatoes by placing them in hot water for a few seconds. Cut the tomatoes in half, discard the seeds and chop roughly. Set aside.

2 Roughly chop the onion, chilli, mint and fresh coriander.

COOK'S TIP
This relish will keep for up to 1 week in the fridge: prepare up to the end of step 3 but do not add the yogurt until just before serving.

3 Place the herb mixture in a food processor with the Tabasco sauce, clear honey, salt and lime juice. Add the tomatoes to this and grind everything together for a few seconds.

4 Pour into a small serving bowl. Finally, stir in the yogurt and serve.

INDEX